FE

The
WORLD
TURNED UPSIDE
DOWN

The WORLD TURNED UPSIDE DOWN

*George Washington and
the Battle of Yorktown*

RICHARD FERRIE

Holiday House / New York

If ponies rode men and if grass ate the cows
And cats should be chased into holes by the mouse . . .
If summer were spring and the other way 'round
Then all the world would be upside down.

From the British nursery rhyme
"The World Turned Upside Down"

For Millie McBroom,
who knows a thing or two about leading
an unruly bunch through life's great battles

ACKNOWLEDGMENTS

Special thanks for those who went beyond the call: Ivette Cortes, Marc Deconink, Diane DePew, Ellen Feldman, Naiyre and Mike Foster, Peggie Gaul, Regina Griffin, Patricia Heidenry, Kathy Hubbard-Ragsdale, Richard Moore, Carolyn and Todd Oronzio, Emily Plishner, Cornelia Read, Bill Reiss, Susan Schultz, Cobb and Bob Stewart

Library of Congress Cataloging-in-Publication Data
Ferrie, Richard.
The world turned upside down: George Washington and the Battle of
Yorktown / Richard Ferrie.—1st ed.
p.   cm.
Includes bibliographical references and index.
Summary: This examination of the events surrounding the pivotal
Revolutionary War battle that led to the defeat of the British
forces at Yorktown, Virginia, focuses on the central role of General
George Washington.
ISBN 0-8234-1402-7
1. Yorktown (Va.)—History—Siege, 1781—Juvenile literature.
2. Washington, George, 1732–1799—Military leadership—Juvenile
literature. [1. Yorktown (Va.)—History—Siege, 1781.
2. Washington, George, 1732–1799.] I. Title.
E241.Y6F45   1999   98-19574   CIP   AC
973.3'37—dc21

MAPS BY HEATHER SAUNDERS
BOOK DESIGN BY DAVID M. SEAGER

CONTENTS

BE IT REMEMBERED!

THAT on the 17th of October, 1781, Lieutenant-General Earl CORNWALLIS, with above Five thousand British Troops, surrendered themselves Prisoners of War to his Excellency Gen. GEORGE WASHINGTON, Commander in Chief of the allied Forces of France and America.

LAUS DEO!

INTRODUCTION

*I*t could have failed. No United States, no Constitution, no Fourth of July. The events leading to the Battle of Yorktown reveal a war that both sides were desperate to see ended. That end came at Yorktown.

For General George Washington, it was the mission of a lifetime. The road in front of him was complex and difficult. If he didn't succeed, he would lose his reputation, his army, and any hope of independence for his country. Nevertheless, he took the gamble, risking it all on a make-or-break battle. What followed was one of the most extraordinary moments in military history.

On October 19, 1781, five thousand British troops under Lieutenant General Charles Cornwallis marched in surrender from their post at Yorktown, Virginia. Legend has it that the defeated British left the town playing an old nursery rhyme called "The World Turned Upside Down"—a fitting tune, for the outcome of the battle changed the world forever.

This broadside popped up all over the thirteen colonies, spreading news of Washington's victory.

How DID IT HAPPEN? How could a new nation challenge the greatest empire of the day—and win?

During the six years before Yorktown, it looked as if the colonies did not have a chance. The Continental Army was falling apart. Men were deserting twice as fast as Washington could replace them. Congress was broke. The country had deteriorated to a state of collapse. Many Americans were ready to negotiate an end to the war without independence.

Yet Washington wouldn't give up. By strength of will alone, he kept the army together until his chance came.

Americans have grown up with the perception of Washington as the man who chopped down the cherry tree and confessed, the stiff, distant figure who rarely smiled in any of the famous portraits and paintings of him. These perceptions do not give a full picture of the man and his deeds.

Washington was a master at using misinformation and trickery during the war. He had a ferocious temper, which he fought to control his whole life. He was as perceptive about the causes of American independence as Thomas Jefferson and John Adams, who were renowned for their intellects.

At Yorktown, the real George Washington shines through. When the hopes for liberty were most in doubt, his inclination to take risks, combined with his passion, commitment, and intelligence, tipped the scales in favor of independence.

THE KEY PLAYERS

THE AMERICANS

George Washington

1732–1799

Commander in Chief of the Continental Army

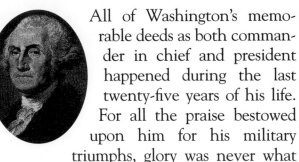

All of Washington's memorable deeds as both commander in chief and president happened during the last twenty-five years of his life. For all the praise bestowed upon him for his military triumphs, glory was never what he was after: liberty was his goal. He wrote, "How pitiful in the eyes of reason and ambition is that false ambition which desolates the world with fire and sword for the purposes of conquest and fame, when compared to the milder virtues of making our neighbors and our fellow men as happy as their frail condition and perishable natures permit them to be."

Nathanael Greene

1742–1786

Major General of the Continental Army

Greene emerged from the Revolution second only to Washington as a strategist and commander. His brilliant Southern campaigns of 1780–1781 helped drive Cornwallis into Yorktown.

Henry Knox
1750–1806
Chief of Artillery and
General of the
Continental Army

A witness to the Boston Massacre, Knox was a supporter of independence from the beginning. His mastery of the siege cannons was a major factor in the triumph at Yorktown.

Benjamin Lincoln
1733–1810
Major General of the
Continental Army

One of Washington's few dependable commanders, Lincoln was captured during the surrender of Charleston (May 1780). After being exchanged for two British generals, he returned to the Continental Army to play a significant role in the attack on Yorktown.

Alexander Hamilton
1755–1804
Lieutenant Colonel of
the Continental Army

At Yorktown, Hamilton was given command of the troops attacking Redoubt No. 10.

THE FRENCH

Jean-Baptiste-Donatien de Vimeur, Comte de Rochambeau
1725–1807
Lieutenant General of the French Army

Rochambeau (pronounced *roe-shahm-boe*) did not speak English, but his considerable experience and skills at warfare, as well as his consistent demeanor and actions, turned the promise of the alliance into reality.

François-Joseph-Paul Comte de Grasse
1722–1788
Rear Admiral of the French Navy

Like Washington, no one could have predicted from de Grasse's (pronounced *grahs*) career prior to Yorktown that he would become one of the major heroes of the Revolution. In 1747, he spent time in a British jail, where he learned information about English ships that he later used to help his own country revitalize its navy—just in time to settle old scores with the British in the American Revolution.

Marie-Joseph-Paul-Yves-Roch-Gilbert du Motier, Marquis de Lafayette
1757–1834
Major General of the Continental Army

Orphaned at thirteen, Lafayette arrived in America at the age of nineteen with scant military experience. He ended up playing a pivotal role in keeping Cornwallis occupied until the trap at Yorktown could be set. He was wildly popular in the United States both during and after the Revolution. He spent $200,000 of his own money to help finance the war and never asked to be repaid. He also took back to France enough American soil for him to be buried in when he died.

Jacques-Melchior de Barras
?–1800
Admiral of the French Navy

De Barras (pronounced *deh bah-rah*) was technically de Grasse's superior, but played a smaller role during the Revolution. He did show up in time to give the allies a boost in Yorktown.

THE BRITISH

Sir Henry Clinton
1738–1795
Commander in Chief
of the British Army

Clinton has been singled out by British historians as one of the most "unfortunate" generals in history. He suffered from nervous breakdowns throughout his career, including a severe one right after the death of his wife a few years before the Revolution began. That emotional instability, combined with tremendous vanity, made him exasperating to deal with, even for his closest friends.

Charles Cornwallis,
1st Marquess
1738–1805
Lieutenant General
of the British Army

To this day, Cornwallis remains a controversial figure in British military history. After the Revolution, he went on to become one of the most successful British generals ever, but many feel his unfocused strategy for the Southern campaigns ultimately cost Britain the colonies.

Thomas Graves, Baron

1725–1802

Rear Admiral of the British Navy

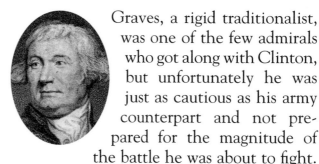

Graves, a rigid traditionalist, was one of the few admirals who got along with Clinton, but unfortunately he was just as cautious as his army counterpart and not prepared for the magnitude of the battle he was about to fight.

Samuel Hood, 1st Viscount

1724–1816

Rear Admiral of the British Navy

Hood was an outstanding commander and great naval strategist, but his frequent temper tantrums made him difficult to work with.

George Brydges Rodney, 1st Baron

1718–1792

Admiral of the British Navy

Rodney recognized the threat de Grasse represented to the British in the Revolution, but due to unfortunate timing and his own personal ambitions, he did little to prevent his arrival. Rodney redeemed himself shortly after the Revolution with a crushing defeat of de Grasse that forever changed the old British naval rules about fighting and reaffirmed the British navy's place as the most powerful on the oceans.

Banastre Tarleton
1754–1833
Lieutenant Colonel of
the British Army

Nicknamed Bloody Tarleton because of his atrocities in the Southern campaigns, Tarleton was put in charge of the Gloucester Point defenses at Yorktown. He has been largely forgotten in British history, but he was so hated in the South that he is still very much remembered in American history.

Charles O'Hara
1740–1802
Major General of
the British Army

A favorite of Cornwallis, O'Hara had the task of representing Cornwallis during the surrender proceedings, after which he had dinner with Washington. Many years later, he was captured and exchanged for Rochambeau during yet another British-French war.

TIMELINE

MAJOR EVENTS BEFORE YORKTOWN

April 19, 1775:   The first shots of the American Revolution are fired at **Lexington** and **Concord,** Massachusetts.

June 17, 1775:   The British take **Bunker Hill** in Boston, Massachusetts, but suffer numerous casualties.

August 27–28, 1776:   The British assemble one of the most fearsome military expeditions of the eighteenth century and nearly destroy the Continental Army on **Long Island,** New York.

December 26, 1776:   Washington orders the legendary midnight Christmas crossing of the Delaware and captures the Hessian guard at **Trenton,** New Jersey.

September 11, 1777:   The British defeat Washington at **Brandywine,** Pennsylvania, and are able to occupy Philadelphia, the nation's first "unofficial" capital, later that month.

October 17, 1777:   At **Saratoga,** New York, British Major General John Burgoyne surrenders to Major General Horatio Gates after the first and second battles of Freeman's Farm (September 19 and October 7). The defeat convinces the French to join the Americans.

February 6, 1778:   France enters into an alliance with the thirteen colonies.

June 28, 1778:   The Continentals fight well at **Monmouth Court House,** New Jersey, but they do not prevent the British from retaking Manhattan.

July 1778:   Large French fleet arrives off coast of Virginia.

August 28–29, 1778:   The first major joint American-French war effort fails as **Newport,** Rhode Island, remains in British control.

October 9, 1779:   The Americans and French suffer another disappointment as they are unable to retake **Savannah,** Georgia, from the British.

May 12, 1780:	In the worst defeat suffered by the Americans during the war, the British capture **Charleston,** South Carolina, after a crippling siege.
July 1780:	Second French fleet arrives in **Newport,** Rhode Island, under Admiral de Barras and is trapped for a year.
August 16, 1780:	Cornwallis nearly destroys the Southern branch of the Continental Army at **Camden,** South Carolina.
October 7, 1780:	Patrick Ferguson's division of British loyalists is wiped out at **Kings Mountain,** a small, heavily forested area in the South Carolina hills.
January 17, 1781:	The despised British cavalry leader Banastre Tarleton gets his comeuppance at **Cowpens,** South Carolina.
March 15, 1781:	Cornwallis battles Nathanael Greene at **Guilford Courthouse,** North Carolina. Greene's army inflicts major damage but retreats before the battle is won.

THE YORKTOWN CAMPAIGN — 1781

May 10:	The British arrive in Virginia, throwing the state into a panic.
August 2:	The British end their attacks and settle in Yorktown for the winter.
August 14:	In New York, Washington learns that an enormous French fleet is heading to Chesapeake Bay.
August 19:	The French army in Newport joins with Washington's forces in New York, and the long march to Yorktown begins.
August 30:	The French fleet arrives in Chesapeake Bay.
September 1:	The British send warships to drive the French fleet out of the Chesapeake.
September 5:	In a climactic battle at the mouth of the Chesapeake, the British navy is defeated and forced to return to New York. All escape routes for the British army in Yorktown are closed off.
September 14:	American and French troops begin gathering in Williamsburg, Virginia, twelve miles west of Yorktown.
September 28:	The 17,000 allied troops arrive at Yorktown, encircling the 7,500 British troops.
October 9:	After finishing the trenches, the Americans and French begin a major bombardment of Yorktown.
October 14:	In the middle of the night, American and French troops storm British positions, severely crippling the enemy's defenses.
October 17:	The British ask for terms of surrender.
October 19:	The British troops, surrounded by the Americans and French, lay down their arms.

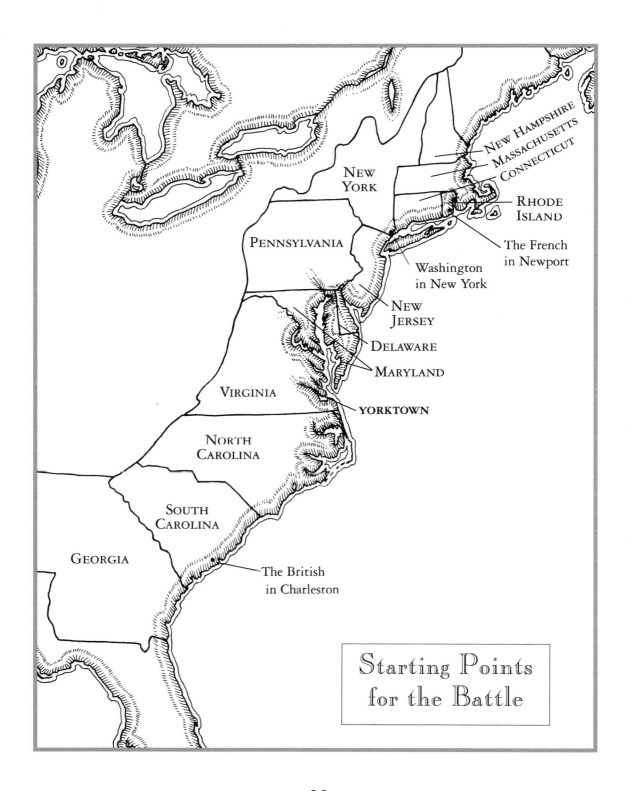

NEW HAMPSHIRE
MASSACHUSETTS
CONNECTICUT

NEW
YORK

RHODE
ISLAND

PENNSYLVANIA

The French
in Newport

Washington
in New York

NEW
JERSEY

DELAWARE

MARYLAND

VIRGINIA

YORKTOWN

NORTH
CAROLINA

SOUTH
CAROLINA

GEORGIA

The British
in Charleston

Starting Points
for the Battle

One

❧

WASHINGTON HOLDS ON

As 1781 began, the United States of America looked unlikely to survive another winter. Holed up in his camp just north of New York City, trying to revive the Revolution, General George Washington wrote, "We are at the end of our tether and . . . now or never our deliverance must come." Winters had always been tough for Washington and the Continental Army. The winter of 1780–1781, while in some respects not as bad as the brutal winters in Valley Forge, Pennsylvania, or Morristown, New Jersey, was equally frustrating for the commander in chief. The core of the British army, 14,000 of its toughest soldiers, held New York City with a force too strong to dislodge, while Washington's 3,500 troops were in a pathetic state, lacking uniforms, decent rations, and money. Many of the troops had fought without pay for a long time, some for more than a year.

For most of 1779 and 1780, Washington had been unable to address these problems except by writing letters. He wrote to friends complaining about the declining enthusiasm for the rebellion, to Congress for money, and to various colonial governors and legislators

No matter how difficult things got, Washington never lost faith in the Revolution. He is shown here personally rallying the troops at the battle of Monmouth Court House.

for supplies, men, and guns. Yet the only response to Washington's requests was more committee meetings.

Many people in the colonies had grown tired of the struggle and of the tremendous disruption it had caused in their lives. If something didn't change, Congress would be forced to negotiate peace on British terms, which meant there would be no hope of independence. The commander in chief knew he had to act. But the continuing shortage of men, money, and firepower kept him locked in a dreary stalemate. "Instead of having everything in readiness to take the field, we have nothing," he wrote to a friend, "and instead of having the prospect of a glorious offensive campaign before us we have a bewildered and gloomy defensive one—unless we should receive a powerful aid of ships, land troops, and money from our generous allies."

For Washington, from the moment on June 15, 1775, when Congress appointed him commander in chief of the Continental Army, the Revolution had been a series of disappointments. Washington was forty-three years old when the war started, a wealthy Virginia landowner. He had some military experience from fighting as a young man in the French and Indian War, but that did not prepare him to lead an inexperienced group of farmers against the world's greatest military power.

Washington realized that leading the Revolution would be the biggest challenge of his life. "Though I am truly sensible of the high honor done me in this appointment," he told Congress during his acceptance speech, ". . . I do not think myself equal to the command I am honored with." He concluded by saying he would take no pay for his efforts, asking only to be reimbursed for his expenses.

Congress could not have picked a better leader. Washington had an integrity that no other candidate possessed. Whatever his shortcomings as a general at the war's beginning, his strength of character more than made up for them. That strength was to carry the country through the bitter days of the Revolution.

The Continental Army performed better than expected in the early contests at Lexington and Concord (April 1775) and Bunker Hill (June 1775). Washington's arrival in Boston shortly after these battles immediately invigorated the army, which began fortifying defenses in and around the city. On March 17, 1776, after an eleven-month siege, the British boarded their ships and left.

The colonists were jubilant. But after the English troops from Boston arrived in Manhattan, they combined with a huge armada just sent from Britain to form the largest military expedition in history up to that point. The Continental Army saw what it meant to have a powerful navy for support and transport. Washington had barely enough time to march his troops to New York to prepare for the coming battle.

The Continental Army was outnumbered two to one. Its soldiers fought as well as could be expected, but a collection of farmers, craftsmen, and adventurers was no match for Europe's most polished troops. When the Long Island and Manhattan battles were over (October 1776), Washington had lost 4,000 men and vital supplies, including cannons, muskets, and ammunition.

The colonists were so stunned by this defeat that many assumed the Revolution was finished. The enlistment term for a good number of the first wave of army volunteers was up, so most headed home. Washington, now with less than 5,000 men and faced with the

The Battle of Long Island established an important tenet: Washington was a master of escape. It seemed certain that his entire army would be captured or killed, but the British awoke the next morning to find their adversary had slipped away.

prospect of losing more after Christmas, retreated all the way to Pennsylvania. Some in Congress and within his own ranks called for his dismissal.

"If I were to put a curse on my worst enemy," he wrote a family member, "it would be to wish him in my position now. I just do not know what to do. It seems impossible to continue my command in this situation. But if I withdraw now, all will be lost."

His men, many without shoes or shelter, were freezing on the banks of the Delaware River. Food ran low. In an effort to raise morale, Washington ordered every officer to read aloud to his troops Thomas Paine's "The American Crisis," which begins with the famous line, "These are times that try men's souls." Less than a week before Christmas, Washington had run out of options.

In this dark moment, Washington came up with a plan to revive the Revolution. The result was the legendary Christmas night crossing of the Delaware River to capture the Hessian guard in Trenton, New Jersey (December 1776).

Historians are quick to point out that Trenton was not a significant military action. Even so, it is impossible to overestimate the impact Washington's surprise had on the country. Overnight, belief in the cause was renewed. Men joined the army in large numbers. Supplies began pouring in.

From that moment on, George Washington realized that the image of his never giving up, of his unshakable belief in independence, was the one thing the colonists could cling to. As long as he and the army stayed intact, there was hope.

He also learned important military lessons from his defeats in New York. His army was not the type or size that could directly take on the

Redcoats. He wrote: "With the fate of America at stake, I see our job as prolonging the war as much as possible. So unless we are absolutely forced into it, our tactics are to avoid a large battle; in fact, to avoid any risks at all."

Despite this decision, Washington reveals in his letters intense frustration at having to fight a defensive war. But one of his strengths was his pragmatism. He knew his novice forces were outmanned and outgunned, and he had to keep them out of situations where they could be wiped out.

As the war dragged on, Washington and his army grew more skilled at their style of warfare. While it rarely won a victory, the Continental Army became more confident with each encounter. The British were both amazed and frustrated at Washington's "ungentlemanly" ability to evade capture.

But while keeping the Continental Army on the move would prolong the Revolution, actually winning the war would take something else. It was clear to Washington that the United States had to have help—money, men, ships, weapons, supplies—that Congress and the country simply could not provide. America's great hope was that France, England's perpetual foe, would enter the war on the colonists' side.

BENJAMIN FRANKLIN had been in Paris for some time, working hard to get French money to fund the Revolution. He'd also been working hard to get the French army onto the battlefield. The French, who had lost to the British in the French and Indian War, were enticed by the thought of revenge. But the Americans had yet to win a major battle. There was concern that the colonists would be unable to hold up much longer. If France did get involved and the United States collapsed, they would be on their own against England. From the French standpoint, the situation was not promising.

That situation, however, was about to change. A large British force under Major General John Burgoyne was on its way to New York from Canada. Another large British force was to move north from New York City, and the two armies would meet in Albany, New York, cutting the Northern colonies off from the South.

The plan backfired. The Redcoats in New York City went to Philadelphia instead of Albany. Burgoyne, who wildly underestimated what his march from Canada would take in terms of men and supplies, found himself surrounded and outnumbered, and after a series of intense battles, he surrendered his entire army to the Americans at Saratoga, New York (October 1777).

The victory at Saratoga was the turning point of the Revolution. It convinced the French that the Americans had a chance. In February 1778, France entered into an alliance with the thirteen colonies. A month later, France informed the British government that it recognized the independence of the United States of America.

Pages 32–33:
Benedict Arnold (wounded at center) had not
yet turned against his country, when his bravery and leadership
won the day for the colonists at Saratoga.

FRANCE'S ENTRY into the war changed everything. Suddenly the Americans had access to both a strong navy and an army with the latest military hardware. While France had been secretly supplying money and weapons to the Americans from the beginning of the Revolution, equipping an army and sending it across an ocean was a more complicated task. It would take months before the French could ready a force and get it to America. In the end, almost one third of the troops that France was supposed to send to the United States never made it.

Having a major power on their side improved the situation for the colonists, but it also altered the scope of the war. The British had to protect not only their possessions in North America, Africa, and India, but also the economically important sugar colonies in the West Indies. Politicians in both France and England believed the West Indies were more valuable than the American colonies and five thousand of the British troops in New York were immediately sent to the West Indies.

Washington believed control of the sea was vital to the success of any war. For years, he had been watching the British sail up and down the American coast on what he called "canvas wings," striking anywhere that suited them: Philadelphia, Savannah, Charleston. With help from the French, Washington would have two ingredients he lacked: firepower to match the British and mobility.

Yet, the first attempts at combined missions were unsuccessful. In July 1778, a large French fleet arrived off the coast of Virginia, heading for New York and a possible joint attack to drive the Redcoats out of the city. But the bigger French ships could not get across a sandbar near Manhattan. The plan was abandoned. Washington sug-

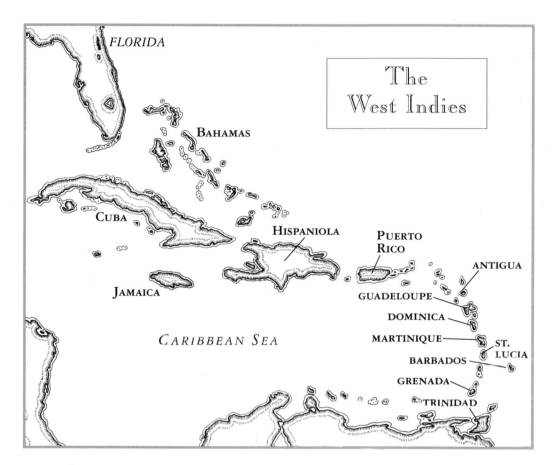

At the time of the Revolution, trade between the West Indies and Europe was thriving. Sugar, molasses, fruit, hardwood, and rope were just a few of the important products traded from the islands. Both France and England knew that whoever controlled the West Indies would have an important source of money and raw materials.

gested an attack on Newport, Rhode Island. The French fleet tried again. This time, a storm disrupted the plans, damaging the ships before they ever reached Newport.

The following year, the French fleet tried once more, this time hoping to retake Savannah from the British. The result: more misfortune. Though the allied forces outnumbered the British, poor management by the French navy caused a series of delays that allowed the British time to strengthen their defenses. The allies were repulsed.

Washington was disillusioned. He wrote Benjamin Franklin in Paris, saying he was "disappointed . . . especially in the expected naval superiority, which was the pivot upon which everything turned."

A second French fleet managed to get to Newport in July 1780, bringing 6,000 troops. In keeping with the pattern of bad luck, the British blockaded the city, and the French forces were trapped. It would be nearly a year before they could move. Fortunately for Washington, however, a much needed boost for the alliance had arrived: Comte de Rochambeau.

JEAN-BAPTISTE-DONATIEN DE VIMEUR, Comte de Rochambeau, was a fifty-five-year-old man with a potbelly and thinning gray hair when he arrived in America. A soldier for nearly forty years and a veteran of many European battles, he was one of France's most famous field generals. Although he liked to be called Papa Rochambeau, he was not known for his tenderness. He had a terrible temper and was a fierce disciplinarian. His troops were the best-drilled, best-behaved soldiers in the Revolution—they had no choice. "I will maintain as strict discipline as though the army were encamped under the walls of Paris," he told Washington.

Rochambeau became a key factor in the success of the French-American alliance. He respected and understood Washington and approached the partnership in a way that appealed to the American general. On his first day ashore in Newport, Rochambeau wrote Washington, "The command of the King Louis XVI, my master, place me under the orders of Your Excellency. I come, wholly obedient and with the zeal and the veneration which I have for you and for the remarkable talents you have displayed in sustaining a war which will always be memorable."

Rochambeau respected Washington a great deal, but there was one major point on which they disagreed: where to launch an offensive. Washington wanted to take New York City, where he had been disgraced. Rochambeau was unconvinced. The waters around Manhattan made maneuvering difficult, and an assault would require not only unquestioned control of the waters surrounding the island but also an enormous army. Combined, the allies could have put together 10,000 troops, not enough to take on Britain's 14,000. With these circumstances to consider, Rochambeau preferred another location for the attack: Chesapeake Bay. Once there, the allies could attack in any number of directions.

Washington had previously considered a Chesapeake offensive but dismissed it because getting his army there seemed too daunting. At the time, there was not much of a British presence in Virginia—a condition that would soon change. Washington also worried that if he left

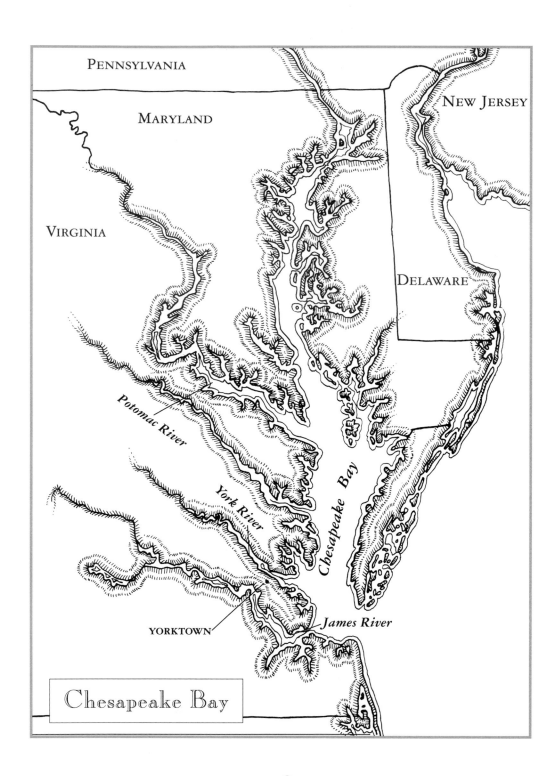

Chesapeake Bay

New York, the British would be free to do as they pleased and might again seize Philadelphia, something Congress would not let him forget.

Rochambeau and Washington agreed on one point: Without a strong navy, neither plan would work. They needed ships before they could do anything. "In any operation," Washington wrote Rochambeau, "and under all circumstances, a decisive naval superiority is to be considered as . . . the basis upon which every hope of success must ultimately depend." The only French fleet in the vicinity at that time was a small one under Admiral de Barras, who was still sitting idle in Newport. De Barras didn't get along with the Americans (or his own countrymen, for that matter) and refused to budge.

Washington was losing time and patience. All the French troops in the world would be of no use to him without a navy to transport, protect, and support them. He implored every important person he could think of to write letters to King Louis in France, urging the fickle monarch to send warships as soon as possible. For if superiority on the water did not materialize, the Revolution would die before the French army ever made it to its first battle.

Chesapeake Bay had such deep waters that the largest of ships could get through. Connecting rivers led all the way through Virginia and up into Maryland and Delaware. Control of the bay meant access to supply and communication routes.

Washington got what he wanted. In March of 1781, seventeen large ships left the city of Brest, France, under the command of Rear Admiral de Grasse, a man who would play a pivotal role in the coming showdown at Yorktown. Finally a navy was coming to help. His spirits soaring once again, Washington began making plans for his attack on New York.

Rochambeau was also excited about the coming of de Grasse, but for different reasons. His commanders in Paris wanted a final decision to this war in 1781. Whichever offensive they decided upon, New York or Chesapeake, the Revolution had to end. Like the British, the French were concerned about their properties in the West Indies and they were considering invading England. Because of this time constraint, Rochambeau knew the first offensive might well be the last one. Therefore, it had to be the strongest one the allies could make.

De Grasse's initial task was to reach the West Indies and secure French possessions there. After that, he had only six weeks to spare in the American colonies. Unbeknownst to Washington or Rochambeau, de Grasse had signed a secret agreement promising the Spanish, who were also about to declare war on Britain, that he would spend the winter helping them protect their colonies in the West Indies.

Although he'd placed himself under Washington's command and would have followed any battle plan that was settled upon, Rochambeau persistently dissuaded Washington from a New York attack. But for all Washington and Rochambeau's maneuvering, the choice rested with de Grasse. While in the West Indies, the French admiral received several letters from Washington telling him of the Revolution's disarray. The situation demanded extraordinary action. De Grasse turned his sights on the Chesapeake, where his ships could do the most damage.

At the same time de Grasse was selecting the Chesapeake, the British had begun storming their way through the Southern colonies, looking for a place to launch an offensive. They, too, now had their eyes on the Chesapeake. The great forces of the Revolution were being pulled toward one spot, headed for a collision that would alter the course of the eighteenth century.

Two

&

The Empire Changes Plans

While Washington and the French were having difficulties getting the new alliance on track, the British were having troubles of their own. Most Britons had assumed the Revolution would be over quickly, and as the conflict dragged on and deepened, they tired of the war. To make matters worse, the French—whom the British considered their real enemy—were involved.

Although the Revolution had started as a dispute over taxes and the right of the "mother country" to govern, it had turned into a war about ideas. America wanted to establish a new style of government. The colonists were fighting for principles.

The English were used to fighting other European nations for competitive reasons. There were well-established traditions and precedents about how these wars worked and about how the countries behaved during the contests. The Americans weren't following these rules or traditions. Washington did not surrender when he was supposed to. The colonists did not give up and go back to behaving the way eighteenth-century convention said they should. Sensing that the tide was turning against it, the British government sent a secret commission to Philadelphia offering to agree to *all* of the

The Redcoats, to their surprise, encountered increasing resistance as they marched through the Southern colonies.

colonists' previous demands except one: independence. Congress refused to meet with the British delegation.

The war was costing the British government a fortune and King George III popularity. In addition, there was the threat of a French invasion of England. Since the British had sent so many troops to guard their worldwide possessions, the security of the British Isles was at stake.

For six years, King George and Parliament had watched the British army chase Washington all over the Northern colonies, accomplishing little in the process. It was time for new tactics, a new theater for battle. He and his advisers decided to turn south, where people were considered more loyal to the King. There, the British thought it would be easier to finish the rebellion.

PERHAPS BECAUSE they didn't take the colonists seriously at the beginning, it was hard to tell if the British were more interested in arguing with one another than fighting the Americans. Since May of 1778, the man running the British military in America was Sir Henry Clinton—already the third commander in chief since the war began. Clinton's temperament made a difficult job even harder. The first thing he did after being appointed commander in chief was ask if he could resign. He had been fighting in the colonies since Bunker

King George III ruled the most powerful country of the time. If the thirteen colonies slipped away, British power and prestige would be greatly reduced.

Hill and realized that this was no ordinary conflict. He complained about the lack of troops available for the job, especially since 5,000 were being shipped to the West Indies. He was concerned, he wrote, about the "impracticability" of winning the war.

Clinton managed to stop complaining long enough to put into motion the King's plan to switch the fighting to the Southern colonies. At first the switch went well for the British. They captured Savannah, Georgia, late in 1778. The city was the southernmost point of the colonies at the time and not known for its revolutionary devotion.

Encouraged by this victory, Clinton decided to make Charleston, South Carolina, the next prize. He carefully planned and executed a grueling six-week siege, resulting in the surrender of the city to the British. Clinton forced the American troops to march from the captured fort "without honors," meaning without music or flags. In eighteenth-century warfare, this harsh punishment was considered a great dishonor and was reserved for troops that had not fought valorously. The Patriots throughout the colonies would not forget Clinton's severity.

The surrender of Charleston was the high point of Clinton's military career and the biggest loss the Americans endured during the Revolution. (It ranks third in numbers as the most significant surrender in American military history.) Fifty-five hundred soldiers became prisoners. The British also captured weapons, gunpowder, and ships. This victory provided a base for the Redcoats, allowing them to strike throughout the South. By the middle of 1780, South Carolina and Georgia were under British control.

It was at this moment of triumph that a crack appeared in Britain's Southern war effort. The main field commander under Clinton was Lord Charles Cornwallis, who had been appointed to succeed Clinton if anything happened to him during battle. Clinton and Cornwallis had fought together in Europe and were friends. Now they were fast becoming enemies.

Cornwallis was an aggressive, hard-hitting fighter who preferred attacking to planning. A favorite with the politicians back in London, he would often write directly to the King's advisers, ignoring or deliberately misinterpreting orders from Clinton.

Clinton threatened to resign several times, saying that if the officials wanted Cornwallis to command, then let him. "I can never be cordial with such a man," wrote Clinton. Cornwallis thought Clinton was incompetent and asked if he, too, could resign. At a time when the two key British players needed to work together, they couldn't have been further apart.

After Charleston, Clinton returned to New York City in triumph, saying, "I leave Lord Cornwallis here in sufficient force to keep it against the world, without a superior fleet shows itself, in which case I despair of ever seeing peace restored to this miserable country." Unfortunately for Clinton, that "superior fleet" had been assembled under de Grasse and was already making its way across the Atlantic.

Also unfortunately for Clinton, the feud with Cornwallis was beyond reconciliation. Clinton gave Cornwallis specific instructions not to do anything that would jeopardize the gains made in the South. Cornwallis could move northward, but only if he maintained control of the land he had already conquered.

Cornwallis was not a man to sit around and wait. He soon struck out on a drive into the Carolinas, hoping to roll up the colonies one by one on his way.

A KEY REASON the British switched the fighting to the Southern colonies was because they were convinced people there were still loyal to the King. Cornwallis and others believed a few solid victories in the South would have people flocking to the British side. The plan was to conquer an area, then have colonists who were still loyal take over and maintain control.

Cornwallis sent two of his officers, Major Patrick Ferguson and Lieutenant Colonel Banastre Tarleton, on raids in different parts of the South. The raiders, especially Tarleton, burned and destroyed villages and towns, killing many civilians in the process. Hatred for the British forces grew with each attack.

Another aspect of the British strategy also worked against them. They began offering freedom to black slaves who would fight for them. The move infuriated many Southern slaveowners, including those who might have been sympathetic to Britain. Any slave who was caught before reaching Cornwallis was either sent back and punished or killed on the spot.

Instead of securing loyalty to the King, the British set in motion a chain of violence that soon consumed most of the South. Bitter vendettas between Loyalists, Patriots, and other groups erupted into savagery. Each group retaliated in kind for whatever atrocity, real or imagined, that was visited upon them.

Horatio Gates, the general who had commanded the Continental Army at Saratoga, was sent by Congress to stop Cornwallis and restore order to the South. In spite of Gates's popularity after Saratoga, Washington questioned his abilities and was quickly proven correct. As soon as he arrived, Gates was crushed by

Cornwallis at the battle of Camden, South Carolina. The Southern branch of the Continental Army was nearly destroyed.

Cornwallis became a hero in Britain. His growing popularity made his relationship with Clinton even more uncomfortable. Cornwallis stopped letting Clinton know where he was or what he was doing. He was committed to putting down the rebellion in the South on his own.

The victory at Camden was the last positive outcome for the British in the Southern campaign. Cornwallis's relentless attacks

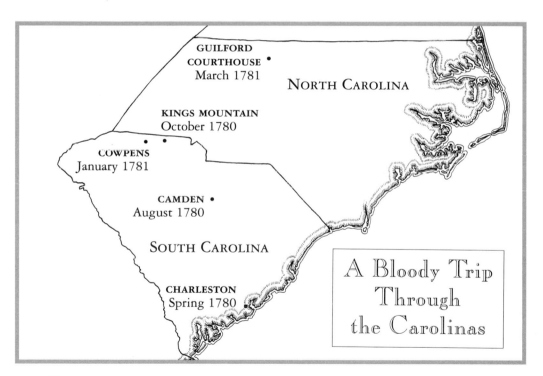

As Ferguson and Tarleton made their way through the Carolinas, raiding towns and massacring civilians, they left the colonists more united against Britain than ever before.

*Patrick Ferguson came to a dramatic end at Kings Mountain. Earlier in the
Revolution, Ferguson had had a chance to kill Washington and did not.
Shooting officers in the eighteenth century was considered dishonorable—that is, until
the Americans started picking off British officers from behind trees.*

and the continued massacres by Ferguson and Tarleton did more to
bring the South together than anything else in the Revolution.
Instead of crumbling to pieces, the people in the South began to
fight harder.

Shortly after Camden came the first of two damaging defeats for the Redcoats. The British raids had so infuriated the countryside that a small army of volunteer riflemen assembled to track down Patrick Ferguson. At a place called Kings Mountain in South Carolina, the Americans slaughtered the British forces. Ferguson himself was killed, riddled by more than fifty bullets.

The second British disaster occurred in Cowpens, South Carolina. This time, the victim was Banastre Tarleton, who had been twice as hated as Ferguson. Although Tarleton escaped with his life, his troops weren't so lucky. Nearly his entire force, a third of Cornwallis's army, was killed or captured.

Cornwallis was furious. He was determined to annihilate the Southern branch of the Continental Army, which was now under the command of Nathanael Greene, the man Washington had wanted in charge of the South all along. Cornwallis was so intent on catching Greene that at one point he had his men unload and burn precious supplies so that they could travel faster.

Finally, in March of 1781, Greene and Cornwallis met at a place called Guilford Courthouse in North Carolina. For most of the day, the two armies traded fire until Greene, seeing that his men were near exhaustion, ordered a retreat. Cornwallis had his revenge, but he lost 40 percent of his army in the process.

The final toll in British lives during the Southern battles was staggering. Cornwallis went from 4,000 troops to about 1,000. Back in London, the wave of losses began to worry some politicians. One member of Parliament said, "Lord Cornwallis has conquered his troops out of shoes and provisions and himself out of troops." Someone else said, "Another such victory would ruin the British army."

Cornwallis, who had so ridiculed Clinton for sitting in New York and accomplishing nothing, had strenuously marched and fought himself into the same state of affairs as his commander in chief: a stalemate. Tired and frustrated, he decided that capturing Virginia might help his cause. He crossed the Virginia state line in spring 1781, leaving British forces in the Carolinas and Georgia exposed to Greene's army—exactly what Clinton had warned him against doing.

❧

CORNWALLIS'S ARRIVAL in Virginia caused an uproar. Virginia was a rich, powerful colony. Many of its residents were important figures in the Revolution: Thomas Jefferson; Patrick Henry; Henry, Richard, Arthur, and Francis Lightfoot Lee; not to mention George Washington himself. Cornwallis felt that if he could bring Virginia under British control, the colonies would be split in two, isolating Washington in the north.

To prevent this, Washington sent a twenty-three-year-old Frenchman, Major General de Lafayette, to battle Cornwallis. Lafayette had been popular with the Americans from the moment he set foot in the colonies. He arrived in 1777 at the age of nineteen, leaving France without the approval of King Louis XVI and the French government. He was full of fire, bursting with enthusiasm for the Patriots' cause. "The moment I heard of America, I loved her," he said. "The moment I knew she was fighting for freedom, I burned with a desire of bleeding for her . . ." Although he had very little military experience, he begged for a chance to fight, offering to work without pay and without troops under his command. Congress was persuaded by his charm and made him an honorary major general.

Facing Cornwallis proved a tough job for the young Frenchman. The army he commanded was in such a pitiful state that he had to spend his own money so that they would have uniforms and equipment. Once the troops were outfitted, he rushed to Rich-

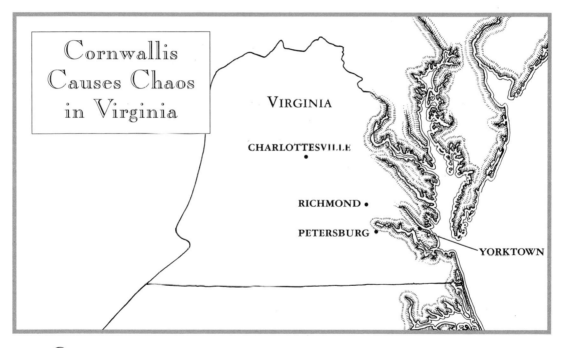

Cornwallis's mystifying path through Virginia made Lafayette and the Virginians uneasy, but had little impact on the outcome of the Revolution.

mond, Virginia, arriving in time to prevent the British army from burning it down.

Cornwallis, however, was not going to be intimidated by some upstart French "boy general." He pushed Lafayette's forces out of Richmond, then turned to destroying farms, houses, and plantations. He sent Tarleton on more of his menacing sprees, one of which almost captured Thomas Jefferson at his home in Monticello. Still dissatisfied, Cornwallis set Petersburg on fire and chased the Virginia legislature out of its new capital, Charlottesville.

Lafayette did not have enough troops to handle Cornwallis's constant attacks and could only follow helplessly while the British army raced through Virginia. By staying close behind, Lafayette hoped at least to give the appearance that he was chasing the enemy.

"Lord Cornwallis' abilities are more alarming to me than his superiority of forces . . ." Lafayette wrote. "[W]as ever advantage taken of him where he commanded in person? To speak plain English I am devilish afraid of him."

The young Frenchman had no clue as to what Cornwallis was doing and where he was going. After following the British all over Virginia, Lafayette wrote in frustration, "These English are mad. They march through a country and think they have conquered it."

❦

CORNWALLIS'S STRATEGY made as little sense to Clinton as it did to Lafayette. Clinton was shocked when he finally learned that Cornwallis was in Virginia. "My wonder at this move of Lord Cornwallis will never cease. But he has made it, and we shall say no more but make the best of it." Clinton continued to hope that the Revolution would fall apart and that if the British would just wait, the colonies would return to the empire. He was against the type of attacks Cornwallis had launched because he feared they would lead to tragedies such as Kings Mountain and Cowpens. He considered it dangerous to split his troops and had wanted them concentrated in one place: Manhattan. Since Cornwallis had forced his hand by going to Virginia, Clinton decided to establish a strong port on Chesapeake Bay. He ordered Cornwallis to choose where one should be built.

There was one serious drawback to the Chesapeake plan: The British would have to maintain absolute naval control of the bay. Clinton knew by then that de Grasse's large fleet had left France and would undoubtedly end up in America. The question was where? And when?

"The success and safety of British troops in Virginia," Clinton wrote to London, "rest with a decided naval superiority. . . . Every precaution should be taken to give me at least timely notice of the contrary being likely to happen, as my ignorance of such an event might be most fatal in its consequences."

He had other concerns as well. Not only was Washington's army showing signs of activity in upstate New York, but the French troops in Rhode Island were also. What was Washington up to? Was Clinton's biggest fear—the long-dreaded attack on Manhattan—becoming a reality?

Cornwallis and Clinton started quarreling again, this time over where the port should be built and exactly how many men it would take to fortify it. Thinking that an attack on Manhattan was certain, Clinton wanted Cornwallis to send troops to New York.

MARYLAND

DELAWARE

VIRGINIA

YORKTOWN

• GUILFORD
COURTHOUSE

NORTH CAROLINA

KINGS MOUNTAIN

COWPENS

CAMDEN •

SOUTH
CAROLINA

GEORGIA

CHARLESTON

SAVANNAH

British Route
to Yorktown

*The Redcoats' brutal trip through the Southern colonies shows Cornwallis's growing
frustration over the revolution. In his private correspondence, his anger is evident.
"What is our plan?" he wrote. "And if we don't have one, what are we doing here?"*

Cornwallis had different plans. Reinforced with additional forces, he had more than 9,000 men. He kept them all in Virginia, leaving Clinton to fend for himself.

By this time, Cornwallis's men were exhausted and dispirited. In August of 1781, arguing with Clinton every step of the way and with Lafayette right behind him, Cornwallis settled into a dying Virginia tobacco town on the Chesapeake called Yorktown. Though no one knew it then, the site for one of the most important battles in history had been chosen.

Three

THE GREAT MARCH

A few weeks after Cornwallis finished his attacks in Virginia and settled in Yorktown, George Washington learned that Admiral de Grasse's fleet had left the West Indies and was en route to the Chesapeake, where he could stay only a short time. Washington was furious. This news was in direct contradiction to plans he'd worked out with Rochambeau at a meeting a few weeks earlier. He'd already begun preparing his troops for an assault on New York. His French allies had switched targets on him.

"I had been hoping for so many months to carry out plans with the French—only to have them thwarted," he shouted during a rare public outburst at a staff meeting. "I wish to the Lord the French would not raise our expectations of a cooperation, or fulfill them!"

Washington soon got control of his anger and carefully evaluated his situation. Although Rochambeau had been pushing for a Chesapeake offensive, from the commander in chief's perspective a key ingredient had been missing: an enemy in significant force to make the trip worthwhile. Now Cornwallis's army was there, and it made a tempting target. Washington realized that if he could trap Cornwallis in Yorktown, it would be a stunning blow for the British.

After months of doing nothing, the American and French troops were finally on the move. Councils of war on horseback were common in the allied camps.

"Matters having now come to a crisis and a decisive plan to be determined on," he wrote later in his journal, "I was obliged . . . to give up all idea of attacking New York; and instead thereof to remove the French Troops and a detachment from the American Army to Virginia."

☙

WASHINGTON TURNED his full attention to the upcoming march. The obstacles that he'd worried about from the beginning with a Chesapeake offensive now required real solutions. How could he move thousands of men in two armies speaking different languages to Yorktown in one piece—and in time?

De Grasse may have decided on the location, but the success of the mission, like nearly everything else in the war, depended on Washington. He took over all planning and troop movements down to the smallest detail. Always a hard worker, he stunned his aides with the seemingly inexhaustible amount of energy he focused on the tasks at hand. Only five days after the arrival of de Grasse's note, Washington had his armies on the move.

Six thousand French troops from Newport, Rhode Island, were waiting in New York on the Hudson River. Together the French and American armies would cross the river at two places, King's Ferry and Dobbs Ferry, less than twenty-four miles from the Redcoats in Manhattan.

On August 19, the armies anxiously crossed the Hudson, boatload after boatload—well over 7,000 men with equipment, artillery, wagons, and other provisions. At no other time during the entire campaign were Washington's men more vulnerable than at that moment. If the enemy attacked, they could have been picked off one by one.

But the British, under the cautious Henry Clinton, did nothing.

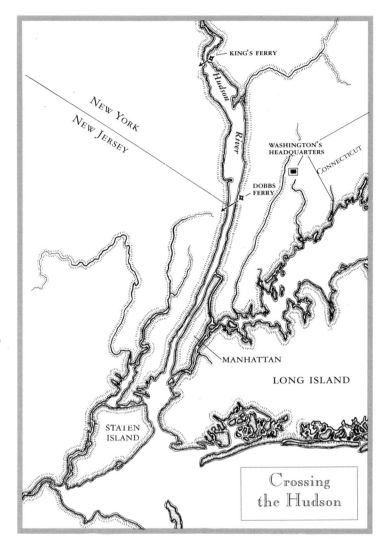

On August 19, 1781, the French Army crossed the Hudson River at King's Ferry and the Continental Army crossed at Dobbs Ferry. Rumors of an attack on Manhattan spread throughout the region.

"Any enemy of any boldness or skill would have seized an opportunity so favorable to him and so embarrassing to us . . . ," wrote one of the French officers. "I do not understand the indifference to which General Clinton considers our movements."

Nothing is exactly what Washington hoped Clinton would do. In fact, he was counting on it. Instead of Yorktown, he wanted everyone—especially Clinton—to think that he intended to attack Manhattan. He demanded that plans for the campaign be kept secret. Even some of his closest friends and advisers didn't know the truth. He pulled every trick he could think of to fool the British, taking advantage of the allies' earlier preparations for an assault on New York City. He had his scouts and spies talk to people in Staten Island, New York, asking about details of the area, as if he were interested in it as a place to launch his attack. He had large bread-baking ovens built there so that it would look as if he expected a prolonged battle. His armies began to gather all the boats they could find and transport them to Staten Island, as if they planned to use them for crossing the waters around Manhattan. The real purpose of the boats was to sail the troops down the Chesapeake.

The deceptions worked so well and the real plans were kept so secret that most of Washington's own troops were confused, having no idea where they were going or for what purpose. Some of them began placing bets on their final destination. Others actually thought their beloved commander may have finally lost his faculties. All this delighted Washington. He believed that if he couldn't deceive his own men, there was no way he could deceive the enemy.

The charged atmosphere affected everyone, filling the troops with hope—something they had not had in a long time. Washington himself was a new man. One of the French officers wrote that the commander in chief seemed "to see a better destiny arise, when at this period of the war, exhausted, destitute of resources, he needed a great success which might revive courage and hope." Even Admiral de Barras, who'd been sitting in Rhode Island for almost a year, decided he would sail for Yorktown "at the first favorable wind."

*The secrecy surrounding troop movements
around New York kept both the French and American
camps alive with rumors and excitement.*

Once the Hudson River was crossed, Washington kept up his dangerous charade by having his men swing around and march directly toward the British in Manhattan, putting the Redcoats on full alert.

It was no use holding back then. Five hundred miles away lay Yorktown. For the commander in chief, it would be an agonizing journey. He had to get the French and American armies there as fast as possible or miss his small window with de Grasse. If that happened, the troops would arrive to find Cornwallis either gone or waiting with a huge army to counterattack.

More troublesome for Washington was the ability of de Grasse to control Chesapeake Bay. It was only a matter of time before the British sent their navy to dislodge him. Just like Clinton, Washington believed control of the bay was the critical ingredient to a successful Chesapeake strategy. If de Grasse failed, then Cornwallis could be rescued by sea.

The uncertainties were endless. The answer to any question could seal the fate of the new nation. Would Clinton attack the armies on the way? Would de Grasse get to the Chesapeake in time? Would Cornwallis try to break through Lafayette's small forces holding him in Yorktown? And what about de Barras? His fleet coming from Newport was small but carried the food, guns, men, and ammunition essential for the siege. What if he didn't make it?

WASHINGTON WASN'T THE ONLY jittery general in August of 1781. In Manhattan, Clinton frantically issued orders and counterorders, had his trenches dug and his defenses reinforced. Washington was coming to get him in New York. Or so he thought.

By then, Clinton had heard reports of de Grasse's fleet. He was one of the few in the British high command who understood the full danger de Grasse represented. He wrote to London, warning, ". . . if the Enemy remain only a few Weeks superior at Sea, our . . . situation will become very critical." But his mistake was that he assumed the fleet was coming to New York. It never occurred to him, until too late, that Cornwallis in Yorktown was the target.

Clinton had become obsessed with Manhattan—more so than Washington had been. He feared that if he took any of his men out of the city he would be attacked and his position lost. He again asked—not ordered—Cornwallis to send troops to help him secure his positions, which Cornwallis refused to do. In his state of anxiety, Clinton imagined that the allies had twice as many men as he did. The reverse was true. Had he moved out of New York and attacked Washington, at the very least he could have slowed the march enough so that the allies would have missed their rendezvous with de Grasse.

Attacking Washington would have required a hard decision, and by this time Clinton seemed incapable of making any decisions at all. An intelligence officer wrote, "There is no spirit of enterprise; the general dullness kills the spark that happens to rise in any man. Washington's present movement from the Hudson is the severest censure upon the British commanders in this Quarter."

Almost from the start, Clinton was getting reports from his spies that Washington had no interest in New York and was really heading South, yet he refused to believe them. He'd already made up his mind that the battle would take place in Manhattan, based on his growing fear and a number of strange occurrences. For instance, in

March, Washington had written a letter to Lafayette, telling him of plans for a combined French and American attack on Manhattan. The letter was intercepted by the British. Clinton was sure that he'd pulled a major coup. One of his staff at headquarters wrote, "The capture of this Mail is extremely consequential, and gives the Commander-in-Chief [Clinton] the most perfect knowledge of the designs of the Enemy."

Some of Clinton's advisers, however, were skeptical of the letter's authenticity. Why would Washington write such a letter without using code to disguise its contents? Was he trying to fool them? Along with the battle plans, the British captured several personal letters Washington had written, including one to his wife, Martha, in Mount Vernon, Virginia, and another to his dentist requesting a pair of pliers to repair his false teeth. These letters helped convince Clinton the captured plans were real. Why would Washington include extremely personal letters along with a note he meant to be intercepted?

Clinton clung to his belief in the face of growing evidence that New York was a ploy. A spy known as Squib sent him a note saying, "General Washington with about six thousand, including French, are on the march. . . . It is said they will go against New York, but some Circumstances induce me to believe they will go to the Chesapeake. Yet for God's sake be prepared at all points. . . ." A week later Squib sent another note: "The Chesapeake is the Object—All in motion." Still Clinton did nothing.

Finally a ship arrived in New York with news that convinced Clinton: De Grasse had been sighted. He was on his way to the Chesapeake. Combined with the fact that Washington and Rochambeau had ridden triumphantly into Philadelphia ahead of their troops (which were halfway through New Jersey by then), Clinton at last saw the full impact of the plan. Like two giant pinchers clamping together, the army from the North and the ships from the South were about to pin down Cornwallis in Yorktown.

Clinton became frantic. "Mr. Washington is moving an army to the southward with an appearance of haste," he wrote to Cornwallis, "and gives out that he expects the cooperation of a considerable French armament. Your Lordship, however, may be assured that if this should be the case, I shall endeavour to reinforce your command by all means within the compass of my power; or make every possible diversion in your favour." To London he wrote more gravely: "Things appear to be coming fast to a crisis. . . . [W]ith what I have, inadequate as it is, I will exert myself to the utmost to save Lord Cornwallis."

But Clinton had waited too long. The door was slamming shut.

WHEN WASHINGTON and Rochambeau rode past the cheering crowds gathered at Independence Hall, it signaled the beginning of much celebrating in Philadelphia. Both the French and American troops, a few days behind the generals, would parade through the city on their arrival. As it was, the two generals were greeted as if the war were over and victory declared. At night, the city was illuminated with candles in honor of Washington, and he bowed serenely to the mobs eager to get a glimpse of their revered general. Unbeknownst to them, their general was a very troubled man.

For starters, the boats that he'd gathered and made ready for the trip down the Chesapeake were hardly enough, and though he'd been promised many more once they arrived in Philadelphia, none were waiting. It meant there could be a delay in getting the troops to York-town. From then on, any delays could cause serious consequences.

A much bigger concern was—once again—money. The army, mostly Northerners, had not been paid in months. Now they were expected to make a difficult march and fight in the South. Mutiny was being discussed. Some troops simply refused to move unless they were paid. Washington had yet another crisis on his hands.

Once more, Washington begged for money. The French were nearly broke and were reluctant to give more than they had already. It was useless to ask Congress. So Washington and his staff scrambled to get supplies and money to keep plans on schedule. "Every day dis-covers to me the increasing necessity of some money for the troops," he wrote urgently to his generals in charge of supplies. "I wish it to come on the wings of speed."

Swayed again by his commitment, not to mention the promise of real coins once de Grasse arrived from the West Indies, his officers and troops remained loyal.

On September 1, Washington received still more bad news: Nine-teen British warships had left New York and were on their way to the Chesapeake. This was an ominous development. These British war-ships might intercept de Barras's small fleet coming down from New-port, or they might get to the Chesapeake before de Grasse. No one had heard from de Grasse in over three weeks. Washington could only pray that de Grasse would hurry. If he didn't, the great Chesa-peake campaign would fail.

The next day, the American troops arrived in Philadelphia. The crowds were just as enthusiastic as they had been for Washington and

*R*eplicas of paper money printed during the
Revolution. The troops wanted real money, preferably
gold and silver coins.

Rochambeau, but the army was in no mood for celebrations. The Philadelphians were stunned by the appearances of the troops—dirty, unshaven, with rags for uniforms, some with no socks or shoes. Washington had the men march straight through the city without stopping and camp outside of town. He could tell by the looks on their faces that these men were not the least bit amused by the cheering of safe, comfortable citizens when they couldn't even afford clothing .

Washington's apprehension was mounting. "I am distressed beyond expression to know what has become of the Count de Grasse," he wrote to Lafayette, who was busy keeping tabs on Cornwallis in Yorktown, "and for fear that the English fleet, by occupying the Chesapeake . . . may frustrate all our flattering prospects. . . . If you get anything new from any quarter, send it I pray you, on the spur of speed for I am almost all impatience and anxiety."

The French troops arrived in Philadelphia a few days later, putting on quite a show. Compared to the grubby, unhappy American troops, the French army looked spectacular. Their uniforms were bright white, with white, gold-trimmed hats and white plumes. Their collars and lapels were blue, purple, pink, or green, indicating which regiments they belonged to. Unlike the Americans, the French troops were allowed to stay within the city, and they charmed the citizens.

Washington had little time for socializing. Every hour counted. Leaving Rochambeau and the French to catch up, he sped on through Pennsylvania, making sure preparations for the second part of the journey were on schedule, all the time wondering where the French fleet was and if they would ever make it to the Chesapeake.

On September 5, a messenger showed up with the announcement Washington had been waiting to hear: De Grasse had arrived with twenty-four warships, 3,000 troops, ammunition, and, at last, money. The troops were already being put ashore to join Lafayette's divisions watching Cornwallis.

Washington was thrilled. "A child whose every wish had been granted could not have revealed a livelier emotion," wrote a French officer who was there when the note came. "I have never seen a man moved by a greater or sincerer joy."

One of the lucky American soldiers who actually had—tattered though it may be—a semblance of a uniform. But he's still missing what soldiers in the Continental Army needed most: a decent pair of boots.

The commander in chief rushed to meet Rochambeau and the other French generals coming down by boat from Philadelphia to join him. When they got to shore, they saw Washington—normally a somber figure—jumping up and down and waving his arms. When Rochambeau got off the boat, Washington embraced him fiercely, telling him of de Grasse's arrival. The French were relieved at the news and astonished by Washington's emotion. Clearly he was sensing a change in the war.

MEANWHILE, CORNWALLIS was slowly shoring up his fortifications at Yorktown. He knew that Lafayette was nearby but lacked the men to threaten him. Unhappy that Clinton had been critical of his battles in the South, Cornwallis eventually forgot about the young French general and returned to arguing with his commanding officer. Washington and Rochambeau continued to move toward Yorktown.

Lafayette's spies were amazed by Cornwallis's lack of energy. "Lord Cornwallis neither pushes his works with rapidity on the land or water side," they wrote. "Like some of the heroes in romance, he appears to despise armor and to confide in his own natural strength."

This changed dramatically on the morning of August 30. British troops were on the beach, building their water defenses, when they saw several tall masts approaching. As the boats moved closer, the troops realized they were battleships and assumed that Clinton had sent a fleet to reinforce them. Excited at this prospect, they began waving at the arriving boats.

But as the ships moved in, the waving stopped. The flags on the tops of the masts were not Union Jacks. These were French battleships, and they kept coming, one after another after another.

The ships' arrival forced Cornwallis to speed up the work on his defenses. He assigned most of the backbreaking labor to the 5,000 black slaves he'd picked up during the Southern campaigns. He began sending coded messages to Clinton in New York, telling him of the situation. Soon he learned of the massive army marching toward him.

In the past, Cornwallis had been renowned for his energy and willingness to go on the offensive. Yet now he seemed paralyzed. He did not attack de Grasse's troops as they came ashore, nor did he try to attack Lafayette's small forces. He was starting to behave like Clinton—fortifying his defenses and waiting to see what would happen next. He lied to his men, telling them that the French navy had not brought any of their real soldiers but unskilled, inexperienced farmers.

Lies or not, the British troops knew they were in a desperate predicament. Nothing Cornwallis could do or say would change it.

WASHINGTON, ON THE OTHER HAND, was feeling confident, and he decided to visit Mount Vernon to see his wife, Martha, whom he had not visited since he had gone to Boston as the head of the Continental Army six years earlier.

The next day, he rode out early, heading for Williamsburg, Virginia, where he was to meet Lafayette's troops as well as the new arrivals from de Grasse's ships. "We are thus far, my dear Marquis, on our way to you," he wrote to Lafayette. "The Count de Rochambeau

During his brief visit to Mount Vernon, Washington's servants were shocked by the change in him. One said it hurt to look "upon a face so changed by the storms of campaigns and the mighty cares which had burdened his mind during more than six years of absence."

was just arrived . . . and we . . . expect the pleasure of seeing you at your encampment. P.S. I hope you will keep Lord Cornwallis safe, without Provisions or Forage until we arrive."

On his way to Williamsburg, Washington received a message that dropped his hopes back to earth. De Grasse's entire fleet had sailed from sight. Cannon fire had been reported in the Chesapeake. No one knew what happened, but Washington understood the implications: The British fleet from New York had arrived and challenged de Grasse. The fate of the Yorktown campaign now rested solely with the French navy.

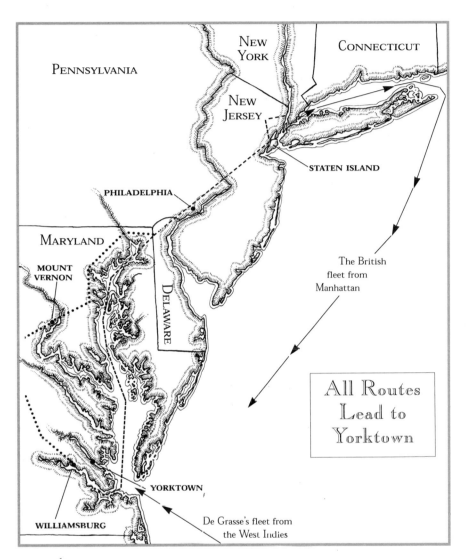

*F*rench, American, and British forces raced to Yorktown, where
Cornwallis was encamped for the winter. The dashed line marks the route taken by
Washington and his army. It splits at the headwaters of the Chesapeake—some of the
troops marched farther down to catch additional boats. The dotted line shows
Washington's route as he made his brief excursion to Mount Vernon. De Grasse
entered the bay from the South, while the British navy—which had taken a long
time to get moving—sailed in from the North.

75

Four

SHOWDOWN AT SEA

On September 5, 1781, one of the most important battles in American history took place—without an American soldier involved, an American bullet fired, or an American life lost. This battle was not fought on land but in the waters off Chesapeake Bay. Over the years, it has been referred to as the Battle of the Chesapeake, Battle of Chesapeake Bay, Battle of Lynnhaven Bay, Battle of Cape Henry, and Battle of the Capes of Virginia. No matter what the name, it is difficult to overestimate the importance this contest played in sealing Cornwallis's doom at Yorktown.

WHEN LOUIS XVI of France decided to send warships to aid Washington, Admiral François-Joseph-Paul de Grasse was promoted and put in charge of the French navy in North America. De Grasse had been fighting the British since he was a boy and once spent time in a London jail after a ship he'd been aboard was captured. Opinion about de Grasse varied throughout the military from "brutal" to "a good seaman" to "too careful."

For more than two hours, forty-three great battleships clashed in the Battle of the Chesapeake.

Admiral de Grasse, the Revolution's most underrated hero, was a tall man, well over 6 feet, and considered to be one of the handsomest men of his day. The legend was that during battle, he grew six inches taller.

Once the American campaign began, de Grasse amazed those around him by the zeal he spent readying his fleet for the mission. In March 1781, he left France and headed for the West Indies. He drove his fleet relentlessly, often towing the slower boats so as not to lose time. He reached the islands in April and immediately began gathering men, money, ammunition, and more battleships for the upcoming journey to the colonies.

The British were aware of de Grasse's arrival in the West Indies but were distracted by internal politics. Admiral George Rodney was the main British commander. During battle, he was one of the best in the English navy, but the rest of the time he was cantankerous and sometimes too preoccupied to keep a close watch on the enemy. Next in command was Admiral Samuel Hood, another capable commander, but he did not get along with Rodney and the two had trouble working together.

To make matters more complicated, Thomas Graves, the admiral in charge of the British fleet in New York, seemed to miss the importance of de Grasse's arrival in the West Indies. Assuming that

Rodney would take care of de Grasse, Graves went back to Manhattan to wait with Henry Clinton. It was, as they soon discovered, an unfortunate mistake.

Rodney finally ordered Hood to intercept de Grasse. De Grasse was not interested in fighting in the West Indies. He wanted to get the fleet to America to help his allies. He kept his distance from Hood, hoping to slip away without damage to his ships.

Hood was determined. Eventually he and de Grasse met in a skirmish off Martinique. The struggle went on for several hours until de Grasse, seeing he had gotten the better of his enemy, broke it

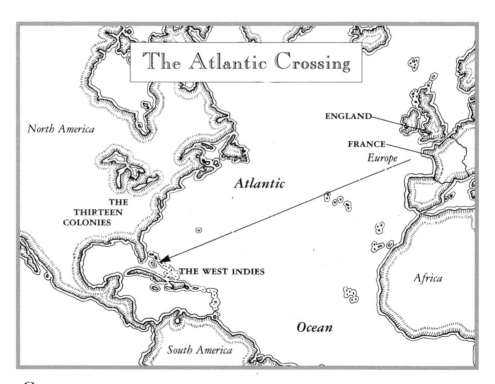

Sailing the Atlantic Ocean in eighteenth-century vessels was an arduous task. The trip from Europe to America took two months, while, because of strong winds, the return trip took one month.

off. He didn't want to risk another encounter if the British sent reinforcements. Before it was over, though, several British warships suffered damage—a factor that would cause major difficulties for the British later on.

This small battle spurred Admiral Rodney into action. He realized the French fleet should be taken seriously and understood the effect de Grasse could have on the war in the colonies. He also deduced that de Grasse's target would most likely be the Chesapeake, not New York City. Because of that, the French fleet had to be stopped before it left the West Indies. Rodney wrote to his wife, "The enemy when they leave these seas will go to America. Wherever they go I will watch their motions and certainly attack them if they give me a proper opportunity. The fate of England may depend upon the event."

Fate, however, was already moving against the British. De Grasse had nearly finished his preparations and had no intention of tussling with the English in the West Indies again. He whisked from island to island, scrambling for the last element he needed: money. He went so far as to put up his own mansion in France as collateral to get silver for Washington's men.

It was in the West Indies where de Grasse made two of the Revolution's most far-reaching decisions. The first was to go to the Chesapeake, not Manhattan, in spite of Washington's desires. His second was every bit as dramatic: He would bring up the *entire* French fleet from the West Indies. It was an astounding gamble. The British never imagined that he would leave the islands unprotected. Nevertheless, de Grasse had come to the conclusion that this war demanded risk and audacity.

When de Grasse had his brief skirmish with Hood, the French had seventeen warships. The British did not expect him to bring much more than that to America. No one guessed the strength of the French fleet that would soon be on its way: twenty-four great battleships. De Grasse told no one of his intentions, and with good reason. The businessmen and merchants (not to mention King Louis) would have been furious to know that he'd left the West Indies without defense. He could have been court-martialed and stripped of his command. Neither did he tell Rochambeau, only hinting in a letter that "though this whole expedition has been concentrated only on your demand and without warning to the ministers of France . . . I believe myself authorized to take some responsibility on my own shoulders for the common cause." De Grasse intended to explode onto the Revolution, coming out with either defeat or total victory. To his mind, there were no other options.

Meanwhile Rodney and Hood were combing the West Indies, eager for a second chance to engage de Grasse. Rodney sent a warning to Graves in New York that the French were coming, but the ship delivering it was captured. By the time the message got there, the battle was over.

More bad luck hit the British. Rodney, who was not in the best health, had a serious attack of gout. He requested and was granted permission to return to England. At this crucial moment, when Britain needed its best commander at the helm, Rodney was out of action. He dispatched Hood to New York to join forces with Graves.

Unsure of de Grasse's final destination and unaware of his new strength, Admiral Hood took off, hoping to beat the French to America. Neither he nor Rodney knew that on August 5, de Grasse's

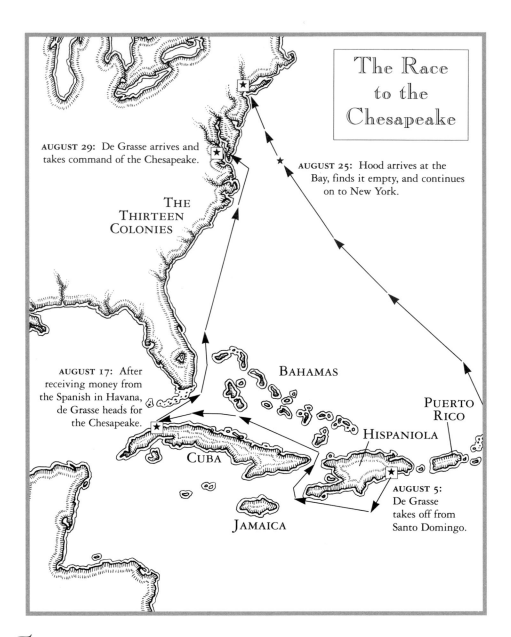

The Race
to the
Chesapeake

AUGUST 29: De Grasse arrives and takes command of the Chesapeake.

AUGUST 25: Hood arrives at the Bay, finds it empty, and continues on to New York.

THE THIRTEEN COLONIES

BAHAMAS

AUGUST 17: After receiving money from the Spanish in Havana, de Grasse heads for the Chesapeake.

PUERTO RICO

HISPANIOLA

CUBA

AUGUST 5: De Grasse takes off from Santo Domingo.

JAMAICA

The Spanish in Cuba gave significant sums of money both to the French navy and the Continental Congress for the Yorktown campaign. As soon as de Grasse secured the cash, he sailed for the colonies. He chose the much feared Bahamas Channel route that passed along the northern coast of Cuba.

armada had left, speeding its way to Yorktown. The race to the Chesapeake was on.

⌘

DE GRASSE DROVE HIS SHIPS to America with the same urgency he'd shown from the beginning of the campaign. He also made another daring decision. Instead of sailing the normal route from the West Indies to the colonies, he took a dangerous, seldom-used one to cut down on the possibility of being discovered.

He led the way commanding the *Ville de Paris*, the flagship of the French fleet. After years of lagging behind the British in shipbuilding, the French had not only caught up with but in many areas had also surpassed the English in their battleship design. The French boats were more durable and easier to maneuver during battle; however, the one area where they still couldn't match the British was in speed. The British put copper plates on the bottoms of their boats, which kept the wood from rotting and slowing down the ship.

Yet even this advantage worked against the British. Hood, from his ninety-gun ship the *Barfleur*, was pushing his fleet to America just as hard as de Grasse was. Because his ships were faster and because he took the more direct route, Hood and the British fleet made it to the Chesapeake several days before de Grasse. When Hood looked in Chesapeake Bay for his enemy and didn't find him, he had no idea where the French armada could be. He turned his fleet to New York City for a conference with General Clinton and Admiral Graves.

Hood's arrival in New York surprised Clinton and Graves and made Clinton very nervous. On the day that Hood arrived, de Barras had taken his small but important squadron of French ships out of

83

Newport. The British had not only lost de Grasse, but they also didn't know where de Barras was headed.

Clinton was certain that the two French fleets would combine and attack New York. Hood tried to reassure the British commander, saying the British fleet "was equal fully to defeat any designs of the enemy, let de Grasse bring or send what number of ships he might to aid those under de Barras." This gave Clinton more reason to remain inactive and reveals the importance of de Grasse's decision to bring up the whole French fleet. Had the British known the firepower being arrayed against them, they would have been more active in changing their situation.

Meanwhile de Grasse and his twenty-four ships of the line sailed into Chesapeake Bay unchallenged and took up positions there. Several warships blocked the rivers leading into the heart of the colonies, sealing any escape Cornwallis could have tried by water. De Grasse knew that hurricane season would start in the Caribbean in less than two weeks and that he would be in serious trouble if anything happened because he'd left the Spanish to defend the West Indies by themselves. He was deeply concerned about a shortage of ammunition, particularly powder for his cannons. He wanted to attack Cornwallis immediately with Lafayette, so he dropped off the 3,000 soldiers he'd brought with him from the West Indies, hoping they could begin the siege.

Lafayette and Rochambeau persuaded him to wait for the approaching Allied armies. Without the combined power of the allies, it was possible that the trap for Cornwallis would fail. With it, the plan's success was nearly certain.

Back in New York, Hood tried to convince Graves and Clinton that the danger in the Chesapeake was very real. Graves considered the growing alarm about de Grasse to be more rumor than fact and was slow to get moving.

But get moving Graves finally did. After much fussing about the battle-readiness of his boats, Graves, on his flagship, the ninety-gun *London*, joined his ships of the line with Hood's. The combined British fleet of nineteen warships sailed out of New York for the Chesapeake. Still unconvinced that the French would be there, Graves wrote that he was setting the fleet's course southward "on the chance of falling in with one of the French squadrons before joined with the other."

No sooner had they started than problems arose from the damage de Grasse had caused to Hood's fleet in the West Indies. Several of the ships began to leak, the worst being the ship called the *Terrible*, which had been using no less than five bilge pumps since it had left the West Indies.

Hood had never told Graves of the extent of the damage. The *Terrible* moved so slowly that the whole fleet had to stop while repairs were made. To his growing anger, Graves discovered that several other ships were damaged almost as badly. They were, in his words, "the shadow of ships more than the substance."

With much hard work, Graves and Hood got the fleet sailing again—at a snail's pace. They reached the entrance to Chesapeake Bay on the morning of September 5. It had taken them three and a half days at the speed of three nautical miles per hour to go 240 miles. This is how the British navy entered the battle that would lose them the Revolution.

At the time of the Revolution, de Grasse's Ville de Paris was the most powerful warship on earth, with 110 cannons on three decks.

IT WAS EARLY THAT MORNING when a lookout on Graves's flagship shouted that he saw what looked like the masts of ships sitting in Chesapeake Bay. A captain scoffed at the lookout, telling him it couldn't be ships but rather the trunks of charred pine trees. The Virginians, he said confidently, often burned them for their tar and left them standing.

Yet as the British fleet slowly moved closer, it became apparent that these were no pine trees. These were French warships, and there were more of them than most British sailors had ever seen in one spot.

Graves was alarmed. At 10:00 A.M. the number of enemy ships in the bay was estimated at fifteen or sixteen. By 2:00 P.M. the count had reached twenty and was rising. Graves thought the only explanation for the huge number was that de Barras's fleet had joined de Grasse's—he did not imagine that de Grasse had brought the entire French force from the West Indies.

De Grasse was every bit as surprised by the arrival of the British as they were to find him in the Chesapeake. The French, too, had been fooled initially. They celebrated when they saw sails approaching the bay, thinking it was de Barras on his way down from Rhode Island. Then they realized the incoming warships were British, had the wind at their backs, and were sailing straight for them. The French were anchored in the bay. De Grasse had just sent 2,000 men ashore to gather water and firewood. Every French vessel was missing at least one hundred men.

In the past, because the British were so powerful at sea, French admirals rarely went on the attack. They approached warfare defensively, interested in keeping their fleet in one piece. Not this time. De Grasse again broke with tradition and took another chance. He ordered every ship of the line to battle stations, determined to hold on to the Chesapeake.

The pipes sounded to get the men back on the ships. Each ship was a frenzy of motion as men hauled up nets, brought up extra rigging and sails, cleared the decks, and positioned the cannons. De Grasse himself could be seen running back and forth on the deck of the *Ville de Paris*, shouting orders across the water as he spurred his ships into the channel. The anchors were cut loose and tied with buoys so that they could be relocated later. There was no time to haul them up.

Once Admiral Graves realized de Grasse was coming out to fight, he gave the command to form a line of battle, though he still wasn't sure how many ships he was going to face.

"Up all hammocks!" was the order that launched the British into action. It was an important procedure, because lashing the hammocks to the wooden rails cut down on splinters, a notorious and painful source of wounds. Nets were fastened to the cannons to catch broken pieces of the masts and spars—as well as men— that fell off during the battle. The ships' carpenters began making plugs from lead and wood to patch up holes from the cannonballs. Last and most ghastly, sand was spread on the decks to keep sailors from slipping in the blood that would coat the decks from the wounded and dead.

De Grasse had his fastest and closest ships leave the bay first, which meant that they would be in the reverse of their usual fighting order. The French were moving so quickly that many men were left behind. One ship, the *Citoyen*, didn't have enough bodies onboard to man the guns on the upper deck. Some ships got out so fast they were in danger of being cut off from the rest.

Many historians have argued that Graves should have tried to pick off the French ships one by one as they came out of the bay. Graves, still shocked by the discovery of such a large enemy fleet, did not press his advantage. Since he was outnumbered, he wanted to make sure his fleet was in the best position possible. He'd also discovered that his vessels were sailing toward a large sandbar, and he gave orders to swing around it. By the time the British had completed the turn and were ready to attack, the French had formed a ragged but effective battle line. All vessels headed for the open sea.

The British had the edge in speed, but because of the wind they were unable to use some of the lower gun ports (otherwise the water would have rushed in). Still, they were in the stronger position to begin the attack.

Yet de Grasse had some important advantages on his side. He had more ships of the line—twenty-four to nineteen—plus 6,000 more men and well over four hundred more cannons. His ships were in better shape than the British navy's. The French also had heavier and more accurate cannons. They aimed for the masts and sails, because destroying these made it impossible for the enemy to maneuver.

Only when the French had their full fleet out and their line formed did Graves appreciate the size of the enemy he was about to

Pages 90–91:
The British, battle line already partially formed, roared down on the French in the Chesapeake. War at sea was carried out by each combatant forming a row of ships that maneuvered opposite the other. When they were in position, the ships opened fire, thundering away until one side gave up.

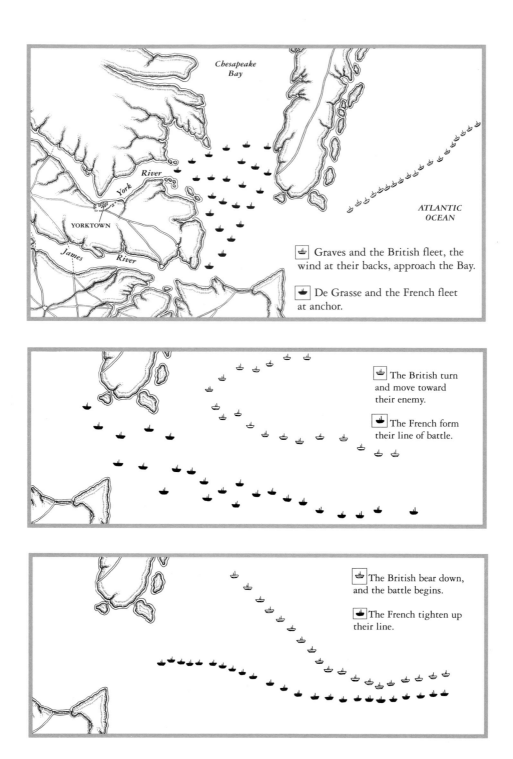

Chesapeake
Bay

ATLANTIC
OCEAN

York River

YORKTOWN

James River

⚓ Graves and the British fleet,
the wind at their backs, approach the Bay.

⚓ De Grasse and the French fleet
at anchor.

⚓ The British turn
and move toward
their enemy.

⚓ The French form
their line of battle.

⚓ The British bear down,
and the battle begins.

⚓ The French tighten up
their line.

strike. Even so, he thought he could take the day and rushed into last-minute maneuvering before the bombardment began. The gunners were already at the cannons, with slow-burning matches in hand and lit.

Admiral Hood paced the deck of the *Barfleur*, angrily waiting for the fight to begin. He couldn't believe Graves had waited so long to engage the enemy. By the time both sides were in position it was nearly four in the afternoon. Not a single shot had been fired. Only a few precious hours of sunlight remained.

At last, Graves hoisted the blue-and-white checkered flag that meant "ye Ships to bear down and engage close." The navies used a series of flags to signal back and forth during battle. The flags were hoisted by the commanding admiral's ship and the other ships looked to them for their fighting and sailing instructions. Unfortunately, flags were a slow and limited way to communicate. The British especially had a difficult time with their signals, using an old system that wasn't flexible enough for the changing dynamics of naval warfare.

Although seeing the battle itself would have been interesting, witnessing the preparations surely wouldn't have been, since it took the ship roughly eight hours to get to the point where they could start shooting.

When Graves ran up the signal to engage, he left the previous flag with a contradictory sailing command flying. The result was confusion. Several of the British ships in the front and center headed into the fight, while others, Hood's included, couldn't engage without breaking the line of battle—now over five miles long—and ending up behind the leading British ships.

It was too late to change course. Hood, the best British admiral in the battle, became a helpless spectator. The fleets closed to about 120 yards from each other, then opened fire.

Hundreds of cannons went off, the force of the explosions rocking the ships that fired them. The first broadside was always the most destructive, since this was the only time when all the cannons were fired at once. Giant balls of metal smashed into enemy ships, shredding the wood as they tore through, obliterating and dismembering the men below and on the deck.

The battle went against the British almost from the start. Two of their ships were quickly knocked out of action. The British captain aboard the *Shrewsbury* had his leg torn off with the first shot. The boat got five holes in the hull below the waterline.

The British *Intrepid* took sixty-five blasts on the starboard side. The *Terrible*, already taking on nearly five feet of water per hour before the first cannonball pierced its hull, was soon listing to one side and had to be replaced in the line.

By the end of the first hour, the decks had become seas of chaos and blood. Smoke from the cannons kept most of the artillery men in total darkness, except for the blinding flash of light as cannons fired. Many of the British masts and spars piled up on the decks, the splintered wood crashing down on top of sailors. Cries could be heard as the debris landed on the men. Those stationed in the cockpit constantly had to run down and either move the wounded to the surgeons waiting below or heave the corpses overboard.

Several of the French boats were hit hard, particularly the *Réfléchi* and the *Pluton*. Almost the entire crew of the *Diadème* was wiped out. Still, it was becoming evident that the French were prevailing.

Because of the confusion with Graves's flags at the beginning of the battle, only twelve of the British ships and fifteen of de Grasse's were involved. De Grasse kept maneuvering his fleet to counter the British advantage with the wind and prevent them from fully reforming their line.

For those who were involved, it was a furious exchange. The men became so exhausted that some ships simply stopped firing at one another, even though they were so close they could talk to each other across the water.

Finally, at 6:15 P.M., it was clear to Graves that the damage to his ships made it impossible to continue the fight. Up went up the flag that signaled cease fire. Shortly thereafter, de Grasse did the same. The great din stopped. The sea was quiet once again.

DARKNESS FOUND THE TWO FLEETS staying close to each other but drifting farther out to sea, away from Yorktown. De Grasse had the French at combat ready all night in case Graves went for a surprise attack. Graves never considered such an idea, but he did reposition his ships "with the full intention to renew the engagement in the morning."

Damage reports began to roll in, confirming everyone's suspicions—the British had been hit badly. According to one French account, "The fleet passed the night in the presence of the enemy in line of battle, the fires in all the vessels lighted. . . . We perceived by the sailing of the English that they had suffered greatly."

For Graves, it was a sobering tally. At least five of his ships were badly damaged. That meant instead of a five- or six-ship disadvantage, he was down ten or eleven. The total casualties from the battle: 90 British dead, 246 wounded. Although the exact breakdown of French casualties and wounded is not certain, their numbers totaled 209.

The situation was so bad that when the sun came up the next day, Graves was in no position to do anything. His armada could barely maneuver, let alone fight. The ships' carpenters were hastily trying to repair the damage before they lost the ships completely. The *Terrible* was such a wreck that it seemed it might sink at any moment.

The sight of his crippled fleet unnerved Graves. Unable to make up his mind on a plan of action, he called a meeting with Hood to discuss strategy. The meeting turned into a shouting match, with Hood accusing Graves of incompetence and Graves accusing Hood of not being active enough during the battle. (The particulars of this argument have never been settled; to this day, historians still debate who did what and who should have done what.) The meeting ended with bad feelings all around and no idea of what to do next.

From the *Ville de Paris,* de Grasse could see the enemy was in far worse shape than he was. He was content to sit tight.

For the next three days, the British argued and the French waited. De Grasse knew he had the upper hand and wanted to keep Graves busy so that de Barras could sneak into the Chesapeake when—and if—he arrived.

It was a rare occasion for a French admiral to have the British in as weak a position as de Grasse did. He wanted to hit them again. He sent a message to one of his fellow admirals, saying, "I have great hopes based upon the damages to the enemy which I can see. I judge by them that they are not as well-outfitted as we are, and by the slowness of their movements that they are not ready for battle."

Finally, on the evening of September 9, de Grasse turned his attention back to Cornwallis. The once lethal British fleet seemed harmless. It was time to get back to the Chesapeake. The French set sail that night.

The next day, the British found they had the sea to themselves. Graves, worried about his fleet and ignorant of Washington's plan to trap Cornwallis, did not comprehend the growing danger the British army was in. Admiral Hood, however, was not so blind. With the alarming absence of de Grasse, Hood sent a stinging message to Graves, asking "whether you have any knowledge where the French fleet is, as we can see nothing of it from the *Barfleur*. . . . I am inclined to think his aim is the Chesapeake . . . if he should enter the Bay . . . will he not succeed in giving most effectual succor to the rebels?"

Which is exactly what de Grasse did, arriving back in the bay on September 10. The French did have one anxious moment when they sailed into the Chesapeake and found another fleet already there. De Grasse immediately sounded the alarm, readying his ships for a second battle.

This time, fortunately, it turned out to be Admiral de Barras, at long last arrived from Newport. De Barras had sailed down from Rhode Island, discovered the battle, then sailed all the way around the warring ships, coming back and slipping into the bay. He had eight warships. The French fleet was now truly overpowering, with thirty-two ships of the line.

De Grasse took full command of the Chesapeake and the surrounding waters, closing off all rivers and ports. De Barras sailed up the York River to unload his precious cargo of siege cannons, food, and ammunition.

Graves and the other British admirals eventually managed to set sail. But when they arrived in the Chesapeake, whatever hopes they had were crushed by the sight of the combined French fleets. Graves had no choice but to return to Manhattan. There would be no follow-up battle. The Chesapeake was lost.

Adding insult to injury, the *Terrible*, no longer seaworthy, had to be torched and sunk. It must have been an ominous sign for the British as they watched the ship burn.

Graves wrote General Clinton in New York, saying, "We met them [the French] on the 5th, coming out of the Chesapeake, and we had a pretty sharp brush. . . . In this ticklish state of things your Excellency will see the little probability of anything getting into the York River but by night . . . the French are absolute masters of its navigation."

Strangely enough, news of the French victory initially did not cause much of a stir. Even some of the participants didn't realize the magnitude of what had occurred. Graves later referred to it as a "lively skirmish." Hood called it a "feeble action." Ironically, King George saw the implications of the disaster the moment he heard the report, telling an adviser, "I think the empire is nearly finished." Washington, too, understood the significance. The one element that could have ruined all his hopes for Yorktown had been nullified by de Grasse's daring action. Washington wrote a heartfelt letter to de Grasse after the Revolution, saying, "Among the many obligations that the United States have gained vis-à-vis the men of the French Army and Navy. . . . that which you have acquired will be profoundly engraved in the spirit of its sons in indelible character, with gratitude and deep respect. . . . You were the arbitrator of the war."

The British fleet was in shambles. The allies could now turn their full attention to crushing Cornwallis. As one French general put it at the time, "Every door is shut tight."

Five
"OPEN FIRE!"

On September 14, 1781, Washington and Rochambeau rode into Williamsburg, Virginia, a few days ahead of the American and French armies. Cornwallis and the British army were only twelve miles away in Yorktown.

Lafayette, who'd been sick with fever for several weeks, managed to get on a horse and gallop out to meet Washington. Washington was delighted to see Lafayette and even happier to see the troops de Grasse had brought from the West Indies. Later that same night, a messenger brought news of de Grasse's victory at sea.

Washington, Lafayette, and Rochambeau sailed out to meet with de Grasse and celebrate his triumph. Washington was amazed by the sight of the huge French fleet, the largest gathering of warships he had ever seen. He and his colleagues were escorted aboard the *Ville de Paris*, and what followed became a favorite legend of the war, retold from soldier to soldier throughout the camp and for many years afterward. De Grasse, a tall man, grabbed Washington, who

*After six years of frustration,
Washington finally got the chance to launch a
major offensive.*

was even taller, kissed him twice on both cheeks, and shouted, "My dear little general!" Those onboard burst into laughter. After their meeting, the guns of the *Ville de Paris* roared in salute to the American commander in chief.

When Washington returned from his trip, he found Williamsburg rapidly filling with troops. The siege was taking shape. Not during the entire war had such a show of force been so carefully arranged and maneuvered against the enemy. Morale improved, helped by the fact that the American troops were finally paid with the silver de Grasse had brought from the West Indies.

Washington gained confidence with the arrival of each new division. "Lord Cornwallis is incessantly at work on his fortifications," he wrote a friend, "and is probably preparing to defend himself to the last extremity; a little time will probably decide his fate; with the blessing of Heaven, I feel it will be favorable to the interests of America."

This optimism did not last long. A messenger brought word that the British were planning to send additional warships to New York. The new fleet would combine with Graves's to try to retake Chesapeake Bay from the French. De Grasse jumped into action as soon as he heard the news. The British had already caught him off-guard once in the Chesapeake. He informed Washington that he was sailing into the bay immediately. He also considered going to New York to battle the Redcoats before they even made it to the Chesapeake.

Washington was enraged. If the French navy left its position, the whole plan would be ruined—right when the allies were ready to march on Yorktown. Washington had Lafayette and Rochambeau write a constant stream of letters, imploring the French admiral to stay put until they could strike at Cornwallis. Finally Washington sent Lafayette in person, hoping the young general's powers of persuasion would do the trick.

The tactic worked. De Grasse held a meeting with all his captains and discussed the situation. The captains agreed with Lafayette. De Grasse decided to stay. He sent Washington a note, saying only, "The plans I had suggested for getting underway, while the most brilliant and glorious, did not appear to fulfill the aims we had in view."

It's unlikely that Washington found the plans either "brilliant" or "glorious," but at least he would have the French navy's essential support during the siege. He could wait no longer nor afford any more surprises. The time had come. He drew up the final battle plans and made the last-minute arrangements. The armies would march at dawn.

"Every officer will be anxious to have his men look as neat and respectable as possible," he specified in his orders. "The Commissary will issue 12 lbs of flour to each regiment, for the purpose of powdering their hair; the men will take care to be well shaven."

On September 28, the freshly shaved and powdered troops marched out of Williamsburg, headed for a date with Cornwallis and the final clash of the American Revolution.

❦

ALTHOUGH HE'D BEEN LARGELY responsible for choosing it, there was no doubt that Cornwallis would have rather been any place else than Yorktown at that moment. When the French fleet had first shown up, he'd remained calm. He assumed that the British navy would save him. His dismay must have been intense when de Grasse returned from the Battle of the Chesapeake not only victorious but—thanks to the timely arrival of de Barras—with even more warships. It was only then that Cornwallis earnestly began to fortify his defenses in town.

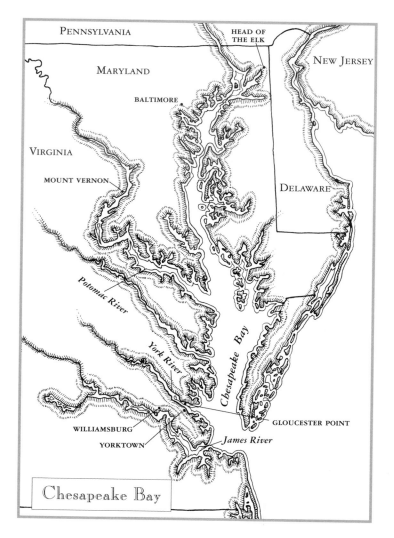

At the time of the battle, Yorktown was a dying, sparsely populated place, well into its decline. That hadn't always been the case. During its peak in the early 1700s, the city had been a prosperous shipping center, bustling with the tobacco trade.

Surprisingly, Cornwallis, the fighting general who always chose combat over any other option, never entertained the notion of attacking Lafayette's weak force. From the moment de Grasse's fleet anchored in the bay, many of Cornwallis's fellow generals urged him to attack Lafayette and escape while he had the chance. Under pressure, Cornwallis tentatively made plans for a strike. But as he was deciding on the timing of his march, a note from Clinton in New York arrived: "I think the best way to relieve you, is to join you as soon as possible, with all the Force that can be spared from hence, which is about 4,000 men. They have already embarked."

The note, as it turned out, was wishful thinking. Graves was still determining which of the damaged ships should be repaired. Yet Cornwallis canceled his plan against Lafayette. He wrote back to Clinton, informing him, "If I had no hopes of Relief, I would rather risk an Action than defend my half-finished Works. But as you . . . promised every Exertion to assist me, I do not think myself justifiable in putting the fate of the War on so desperate an attempt."

By this time, the British could hear the pounding footsteps as the allied troops closed in. Cornwallis tried everything to shore up his defenses. The Redcoats had several small ships and frigates docked nearby, and he ordered most of the cannons removed and placed in strategic areas around the town. He also sank twelve of the ships to help block attack from the rear, making it difficult for French warships to come any closer than they already were.

One of the most daring plots the British tried was to launch several fire ships toward the French fleet in hopes they would be forced to move farther away from Yorktown, opening an escape route for the trapped troops. Late at night, these ships were loaded with tar, sulfur, and whatever flammable materials the Redcoats could spare. Under cover of darkness, they were sailed down the York River, ready to ignite as close to the French battleships as possible. One of the boats burst into flames too early, however, alerting the French to the danger. The fires from the burning ships were enormous, visible from nearly ten miles away. Although several of de Grasse's ships ran aground scurrying out of the way of the fiery vessels, no serious damage resulted.

The failure of the fire ships darkened an already pessimistic mood in the British camp. Cornwallis tried to convince his troops that the cannons they had taken from the ships would be an immense help during the fight. He continued to insist that he could hold out for six weeks, which was more than enough time for a rescue effort to arrive from New York. But whatever Cornwallis may have said, his men could sense the truth. "We get terrible provisions now," one of the soldiers wrote as the Americans and French closed in, "putrid ship's meat and wormy biscuits that have spoiled on the ships." Another was more foreboding. He wrote about the coming of a "fatal storm, ready now almost to burst upon our heads."

As the combined French and American troops worked their way from Williamsburg to Yorktown, Washington raced ahead to survey the scene and make detailed maps of the defenses Cornwallis had put up to stop him. He did not like what he found. The British had two well-developed lines surrounding the city, each anchored down with several redoubts. With his troop strength at nearly 18,000—twice as large as Cornwallis's—Washington was confident he could eventually force the British to quit the fight. The question was, did he have enough time? If the siege took too long, Washington risked losing de Grasse. The admiral was already making plans to return to the West Indies. The other factor that preyed on Washington's mind was the inevitable loss of life it would cost to wear down such formidable positions. The harder he pressed to finish off the enemy, the higher the price the American and French soldiers would pay in blood.

To minimize allied bloodshed, he decided to bring every single cannon he had to the front of the line and bombard the Redcoats into surrender. He was determined not to allow a single British soldier through from any possible escape route. There would be no full frontal assault from the allied troops until the last cannon was in place and firing away. If he could help it, Washington wouldn't engage his troops at all. After a long, difficult war, filled with unusual tactics and maneuvers, the siege of Yorktown would follow standard rules of warfare.

As the marching troops neared their target, they split into two groups. The Americans headed to the south of Yorktown, the French to the north. The latest order from Washington was a grim one, revealing the commander in chief's frame of mind: If the British came out to fight, there would be no shooting. He wanted the armies to settle things in hand-to-hand combat with bayonets.

Pages 108–109
Redoubts—like this one still standing in Yorktown today—
are large earthworks lined with sharp-pointed logs. Properly constructed,
they could absorb much of the impact from
cannonballs. They also acted as barriers against assault troops.

It was an important message, for after suffering through the war without the kind of army he needed to go on the offensive, Washington was about to wield a professional army against Cornwallis. It wasn't just the presence of the French soldiers that had changed the equation. The Continental Army, after six years of surviving in abysmal conditions, had hardened into a core of experienced, disciplined soldiers who knew how to fight. In the early battles, they'd faltered whenever the British had advanced with their bayonets. Some had no idea of how to use them. Not any longer. This was a real army. Washington wanted the consequence of this evolution made clear at Yorktown. There would be no draws, no partial victories. This battle would be the last.

The armies first sighted Yorktown around three in the afternoon. Later that evening, the men began setting up camps—or at least finding reasonably dry and warm places to sleep. They'd moved so quickly that tents and other supplies hadn't arrived yet. The huge, heavy cannons were still being lugged across the sandy and sometimes swampy landscape. The first night was not a comfortable one for the exhausted soldiers. Washington himself was forced to sleep under a mulberry tree.

The next day, the troops began making camp in earnest. The guns were still lagging to the rear, so that much of the backbreaking, exhausting trench digging couldn't begin. During the day, the British fired upon the armies, and there were brief skirmishes at some locations, but mostly both sides were waiting. Once the big guns arrived, the allied troops planned to fortify their positions for the initial cannonade of the British first line of defense.

The following morning, Washington and his troops woke to a surprising development: Cornwallis had abandoned his first line overnight, pulling all the troops behind the second line near the town. The move stunned Washington and Rochambeau. The French general said, "The enemy ought to have kept these redoubts until they were forced to abandon them. . . . It would have compelled us to feel our way, and would have held us in doubt . . . instead of leaving us masters of all the approaches to the place."

Many of Cornwallis's fellow officers were also critical of the move. But Cornwallis, after receiving another note from Clinton promising a rescue fleet of twenty-three ships and 5,000 men, decided to pull his troops in and strengthen his last line of defense while waiting for help.

Clinton, the twenty-three ships, and the 5,000 men still hadn't left New York, nor were they even close to doing so.

No matter what he thought Clinton's intentions were, Cornwallis's desertion of his first line of defense was criticized harshly then and has been since. The abandonment of those critical lines shaved weeks off the time the allied troops would have spent to take them and saved the lives of many of Washington's men.

Washington decided that his first line of attack would include his enemy's deserted defenses. Half the work of building the trenches was already done. He had his men dig tunnels between the redoubts and reshape the ground for placement of siege cannons. This new spot would give his men a tremendous position from which to attack the enemy.

Despite this gift from Cornwallis, Washington became anxious while he waited for the big guns. He moved constantly from position

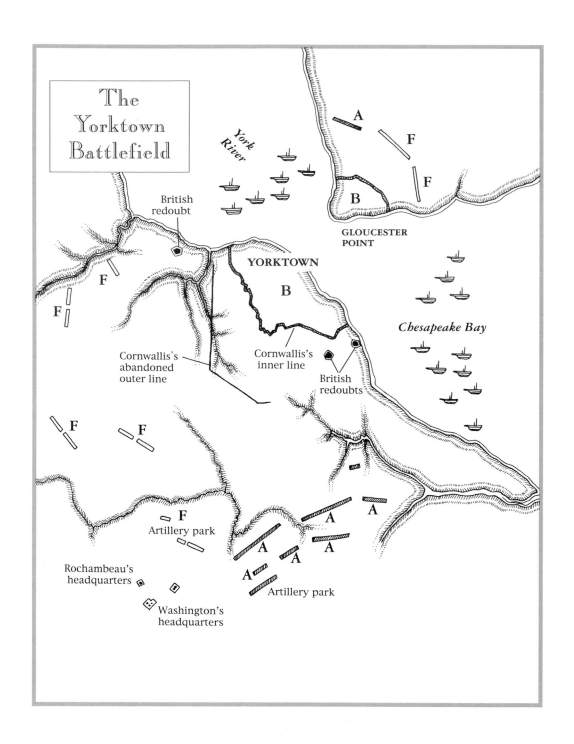

The
Yorktown
Battlefield

York River

A

F

F

British redoubt

B

GLOUCESTER POINT

YORKTOWN

F

B

F

F

Cornwallis's abandoned outer line

Cornwallis's inner line

British redoubts

Chesapeake Bay

F

F

F

Artillery park

A

A

A

A

A

A

A

A

Rochambeau's headquarters

Artillery park

Washington's headquarters

to position, exhorting his men to work faster. "The present moment will decide American independence," he proclaimed in orders heard by every man, ". . . the passive conduct of the enemy argues his weakness . . . the liberties of America and the honor of the Allied Arms are in our hands."

The British stepped up their cannon fire on the troops, trying to disrupt construction of the trenches as much as they could. To save on ammunition, Cornwallis had them fire flash powder, which wasn't really cannon shot, but since the allied troops couldn't tell the difference until impact, they had to duck for cover just the same.

In spite of the delays, the American and French armies continued their work at a breathless pace. The spirits of the troops rose each day. Once the line was finished, the cannons would do the work. The British would get an explosion of artillery like they'd never had before.

In fact, the mood in the allied camps was so optimistic that some men became careless. A soldier jumped up on one of the first works finished by the Americans and taunted the British to try to hit him with their cannons. According to a captain who witnessed what followed, the man "had escaped longer than could have been expected, and, growing fool-hardy, brandished his spade at every ball that was fired, till, unfortunately, a ball came and put an end to his capers."

By the end of September 1781, French and American troops had completely surrounded Cornwallis in Yorktown.

Even Washington sometimes seemed too confident. Being such a tall man with a distinctive bearing, he made an easy target. On a number of occasions, cannonballs exploded around him, sending everyone scrambling for cover. The American general, however, appeared unfazed, and in one instance simply removed his hat, shook off the sand and dirt, then continued his inspection.

Finally the hard work began to produce results. Lines of heavy artillery were forming to the rear of the troops, with some closer to the front near readiness as well. Although many generals were pushing him to fire the guns right away, Washington held fast on his promise not to fire a single cannon until every gun was in place.

On October 5, Washington made a surprise decision of his own. He wanted a parallel dug in front of his rapidly forming first line. This parallel would be much closer to the Redcoats. Not only that, he wanted it built in one night.

His engineers and miners scouted out the area that evening, finding the best spot for the line. Washington himself moved among the men in a black cape, his face hidden from view. Several of the soldiers did not learn it was Washington until much later and were amazed that the commander in chief would expose himself so close to the enemy, only 200 yards away. But Washington would leave no detail unchecked. Everything had to be perfect.

Forty-three hundred men crept silently across the field the next night and began digging a new advance line. The planning and execution went smoothly. On the following morning, the British woke to find a new trench, over 2,000 yards long, staring them in the face. Washington and the allies had tightened their grip.

THE MOMENT EVERYONE had been waiting for came near three o'clock in the afternoon of October 9. The French, cannons in place, ammunition loaded and ready, opened fire on British positions in Yorktown. Two hours later, the Americans did the same, with Washington firing the first cannon. The onslaught had begun.

The toll upon the British was immediate and devastating, far more than Cornwallis seemed to have anticipated. He wrote, "The fire continued incessant from heavy cannon . . . until all our guns were silenced, our work much damaged and our loss of men considerable." A fellow soldier wrote, "It will be impossible to account for the number killed and wounded . . . I must content myself with observing that the slaughter was great."

Once Washington fired the first cannon, he kept them roaring all night. During the first twenty-four hours of unleashing the heavy artillery, the allies launched over 3,600 shells. To the British soldiers huddled pathetically in their trenches, it was as if the sky were exploding, raining down a sea of metal, death, and destruction. Washington had the men aim at houses they thought Cornwallis might be in, hoping to bring him to a quick surrender. The French gunners were deadly accurate, the best in Europe, and had no trouble hitting their targets. The Americans, at Henry Knox's direction, also did well, considering their antiquated equipment and lack of experience. By the following morning, four more batteries had joined in the pounding, making it over fifty guns thundering away at the British.

*Although the procedure of firing the first cannonball was
usually ceremonial, the commander in chief (next to cannon) helped the
Allied cause. A soldier on the scene wrote later:
"The first gun which was fired went through one [house] where many of
the officers were at dinner, and over the tables,
discomposing the dishes, and either killed or wounded the
one at the head of the table."*

116

Cornwallis's letters to Clinton, which now had to be slipped out through the back country or snuck aboard small trading ships, became increasingly hopeless. Cornwallis realized only a direct attack by both land and sea would save him. He urged Clinton to move and move quickly. By the time he was finished writing one such letter to New York, he had to add a post script that read: "Since the above was written we have lost Thirty Men." The next day, while Cornwallis was watching the bombardment continue, a cannonball ripped the head off the messenger standing next to him.

Cornwallis also decided that provisions were so low that he could no longer afford to feed the former slaves who'd done the bulk of the hard work building up the defenses. They'd been promised freedom for their efforts. Instead, they were forced out into the oncoming gunfire of the allies. In a war that was being fought for the ideals of liberty, equality, and freedom, the treatment of blacks in the Revolution made a shameful footnote that foretold of a divisive, destructive conflict to come for the new nation.

On the other side, Washington was pleased with the battle so far and wanted to risk opening another parallel still closer to the British. It was to be done according to the same procedure as the first, meaning everything had to be finished in one night. As before, the meticulous planning paid off. The new parallel was open. But this time, there was a hitch. The British had two redoubts—the last ones before the main line of defense—that prevented Washington from forming his line all the way around. Without hesitating, Washington decided to storm the redoubts and drive the British out in hand-to-hand combat.

The details were worked out quickly, with the commander in chief timing things down to the second. Once he was satisfied with the plan, he ordered the cannons to be concentrated on the redoubts, softening them up for the coming attack.

Two teams, one French, one American, of 250 men each were chosen to carry out the assault. The French would take care of Redoubt No. 9; the Americans, under the command of Lafayette, would finish off Redoubt No. 10. Lafayette chose Alexander Hamilton to lead the charge and made a wager with his French counterpart that the Americans would be in their redoubt first.

In the fog and chilly night air of October 14 the storming of redoubts began. The men were under orders not to shoot until they were actually inside the enemy works for fear of alerting the Redcoats to the attack. Washington wouldn't even allow them to load bullets in their guns. Instead, each soldier attached a long, deadly bayonet to his musket. Cold steel was the weapon of choice.

The first wave of men had the toughest and most dangerous job. They would carry axes and picks to cut down the sharp logs and spikes the British had placed around the redoubts. The problem was that as soon as the chopping began, the British soldiers would undoubtedly hear and begin shooting. That meant the troops coming behind had to be up the wall and over quickly. Surprise was the key.

At 7:00 P.M. sharp, the mission began. The men ran across the field in absolute silence until they reached the redoubt. As they feared, once the chopping started, several British soldiers began to fire down on the attackers. "Rush on, boys!" someone shouted from the front. The sound of gunfire spurred on the rest of the troops. They leaped over the first bunch still hacking away at the spikes. The Americans began slashing at their enemies with bayonets, frantically trying to get up and over the wall. More Redcoats realized what was going on and came to help. A deadly hail of bullets slammed into the Americans racing up the wall.

But the surprise had been effective, the allies determined. Within a matter of moments, the Americans swept over the wall, crashing down onto the British inside. After a few more moments of fierce hand-to-hand fighting, the enemy began to surrender and the British commander of the redoubt was made prisoner.

Lafayette did not forget his bet. As soon as he was in the redoubt, he sent an aide asking his fellow French commander, "I am in my redoubt. Where are you?" The reply came in a few minutes: "Tell the Marquis I am not in mine, but will be in five minutes."

The British put up a tougher fight against the French in Redoubt No. 9, but the outcome was just as satisfying. Both redoubts were taken.

"The work is done, and well done," Washington said to his officers.

The next morning, the trenches connecting the redoubts to the new parallel were finished. The relentless shelling began again, this time from closer than ever.

Pages 120–121:
*Storming the redoubts meant going directly
into enemy fire and always ended with hand-to-hand combat.
Washington was impressed by the show of bravery during the
storming of the redoubts. One wounded soldier, William Brown
of Connecticut, was awarded a new medal for valor—
the Purple Heart.*

ONE OF CORNWALLIS'S later messages to Clinton during the siege contained a dire warning: "If you cannot relieve me very soon, prepare to hear the worst." But in reality, Cornwallis, with the storming of the redoubts and with Washington and his guns sitting on top of him, probably did not believe he could be rescued at this point. The end would not be long in coming.

With the most disastrous defeat of his career looming closer, Cornwallis decided on some desperate actions.

The first was a feeble attempt to charge the allies' line. He had a small band of men make a sneak attack very late at night to spike cannons and ruin as many guns as possible. The British soldiers, showing as much bravery as the American and French troops had earlier, made a gallant attempt and did manage to kill several allied soldiers as well as spike a number of cannons. But the spiked cannons were repaired quickly and, to the horror of the British, even more cannons were soon hammering away at them. One soldier wrote in his journal: "With the dawn the enemy began to fire heavily, as he had not done so before . . . so fiercely as though the heavens would split. . . . Now we saw what was to happen to us."

Under mounting pressure from his young officers, Cornwallis next ordered a risky escape attempt. Directly across the York River was the village of Gloucester Point. Cornwallis had put a small force under Tarleton to guard it so that the enemy could not come at him from that position. But Washington had planned well for Gloucester Point, too. A sizable force cut off any retreat through the village. Washington also made sure the cannons did not neglect the British troops stationed there. They got their share of the bombardment.

The British decided they had a better chance of breaking through Gloucester Point than through Washington's main defense. Cornwallis gathered all the small boats he could find—those he hadn't already sunk to keep the French away, and those that weren't badly damaged by the unceasing cannonade—for an escape attempt. Late on the night of October 16, his men began boarding the boats and crossed the river to Gloucester Point.

The first load made it across before an autumn squall blew up around midnight, making further crossings impossible. The boats were battered; some were blown all the way up the river and captured by American forces. Finally Cornwallis gave up and brought back the men who had made it over. By then, it was daybreak and the French, who had spotted the Redcoats, were firing mercilessly at them as they ran back into their bunkers. Tarleton, who was becoming increasingly critical of Cornwallis's decision making, later wrote, "Thus expired the last hope of the British Army."

WHILE THE SHELLING INTENSIFIED in Virginia, the British military in Manhattan tried to figure out some way to help their fellow soldiers. Clinton continued to write hopeful letters to Cornwallis, promising he was on his way with ships and troops. But each letter arrived with a later date for rescue. The British admirals continued to argue among themselves about who had lost the Chesapeake sea battle and why. It was proving impossible to put the British navy back together in time.

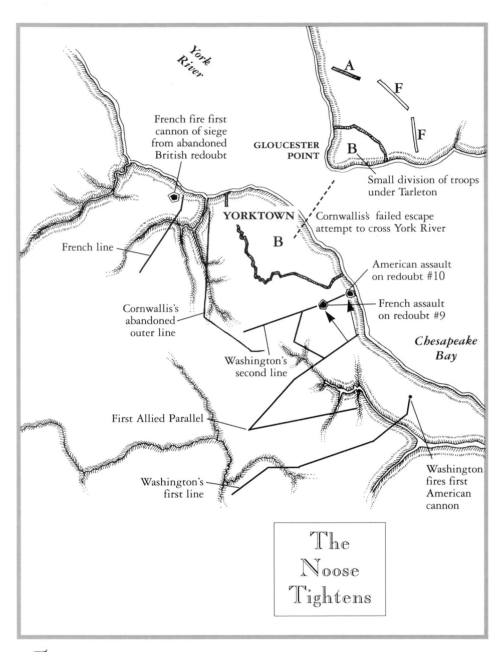

York River

French fire first
cannon of siege
from abandoned
British redoubt

A

F

F

**GLOUCESTER
POINT**

B

Small division of troops
under Tarleton

YORKTOWN

B

Cornwallis's failed escape
attempt to cross York River

French line

American assault
on redoubt #10

French assault
on redoubt #9

Cornwallis's
abandoned
outer line

*Chesapeake
Bay*

Washington's
second line

First Allied Parallel

Washington's
first line

Washington
fires first
American
cannon

The
Noose
Tightens

The assault on redoubts No. 9 and 10 brought the allies uncomfortably close
to the British in Yorktown. With the enemy moving in, Cornwallis ordered the
ill-fated escape attempt across the York River.

Starting from early September, Clinton had held no less than thirteen councils of war, endlessly debating what to do. Part of the problem was that the British ships were in a terrible state. It took Graves and the navy four days to decide what repairs were needed. They seemed unable to estimate how long the repairs would take. Target dates came and went while hope for Cornwallis slipped away.

As if things weren't bad enough, King George's son, Prince William, arrived in New York for a birthday visit. For the next two days, everyone spent time entertaining the young royal. Clinton himself escorted the prince on walks and had him attend troop inspections.

Once the prince left, Clinton went back to holding councils and coming up with numerous plots to save Cornwallis. The plans varied from improbable to dangerous. They included sailing into the Chesapeake and dropping off troops, or dropping off troops somewhere else while the navy attacked de Grasse. Clinton even considered a counterattack against Philadelphia in the hopes that Washington would abandon Yorktown to save the city.

More bad news arrived: There was not enough lumber to repair the ships, nor the right type of gunpowder for the cannons. The sailing date was postponed yet again.

After much consternation, the British managed to get armies onboard the ships. Wind shifts delayed departure two more days. Finally, on October 19, more than six weeks after the Chesapeake battle, Graves, Clinton, and company cleared New York, hoping to relieve Cornwallis.

On that very day, in the city of Yorktown, the world was being turned upside down.

Six

"The Play, Sir, Is Over"

Washington greeted the arrival of October 17, 1781, with one of the heaviest barrages of the siege thus far. The morning thundered with hundreds of explosions as the allies shelled the Redcoats with every cannon available.

In Yorktown, Cornwallis stood in his bunker, surveying the damage. Many of the men could tell by his grim look that he'd already reached a decision. The previous night's failure to escape across the York River made the situation hopeless. He and his fellow officers held one final council of war. Of the nearly 9,000 British troops present when the siege started, only 3,200 were able to carry on the fight. At any moment, they expected de Grasse would begin firing his cannons from the warships, adding to the devastation. To hold out any longer meant certain doom.

There was no other choice.

Around 10:00 A.M., an American soldier firing away at the Redcoats saw "a drummer mount the enemy's parapet and beat a parley, and immediately an officer, holding up a white handkerchief, made his

On a cool October afternoon, Washington (on the white horse) watched the British presence in the thirteen colonies come to an end—only fifteen miles from where it had begun nearly two centuries earlier in Jamestown.

127

appearance outside their works. The drummer accompanied him, beating. Our batteries ceased." Another soldier who heard the drummer wrote: "He might have beat till Doomsday, if he had not been sighted by men in the front lines. The constant firing was too much for the sound of a single drum; but when the firing ceased, I thought I had never heard a drum equal to it—the most delightful music to us all."

The allied soldiers began shouting with joy, clapping wildly and embracing one another in exhilaration. To everyone's surprise, Washington charged up and down the lines on his horse, ordering the soldiers back into combat readiness. The battle was not won yet, and he didn't want it jeopardized by premature celebration. "Posterity will do the huzzahs for us!" he shouted to his troops.

After days of near constant shelling, the battlefield fell eerily silent, except for quiet drumming as British messengers made their way across the ravaged terrain. Once they reached the American line, they were immediately taken to Washington.

A note from Cornwallis read as follows:

Sir
I propose a cessation of hostilities for twenty-four hours, and that two officers may be appointed by each side to meet at Mr. Moore's house to settle terms for the surrender of the posts of York & Gloucester.

I have the honour to be
Sir
your most obedient &
most humble Servant
Cornwallis

Washington spoke calmly to his men, making arrangements for something he'd never been involved with before: a peace summit. Whatever emotions he felt are known only to him. He didn't write anything down except for official reports of the proceedings.

A reply to Cornwallis's message was cautiously crafted. Even though his foe was on the brink of collapse, Washington was still concerned. He didn't want a tedious, dragged out surrender process that might give enough time for the British navy to come to the rescue. "An ardent desire to spare the further effusion of blood," he stated in his communication to Cornwallis, "will readily incline me to listen to such terms for the surrender of your posts and garrisons of York and Gloucester as are admissible."

He wasn't going to wait long. He gave the Redcoats a two-hour time limit in which to respond. As soon as the British messenger and drummer made it back to their lines, the cannons opened fire to let Cornwallis know he meant things to proceed quickly.

Cornwallis answered Washington soon enough, but there were problems with his proposal—problems severe enough to threaten the shaky truce. One sticking point was the British insistence that deserters, Tories, and other Americans who had fought against the allied forces should be set free. Washington refused to comply.

But the real issue bogging down the surrender was the point of marching from Yorktown without honors. No one had forgotten that less than two years before Clinton forced the Americans under General Benjamin Lincoln to march without honors from Charleston, South Carolina, after that city had surrendered. Many of those Americans—including Benjamin Lincoln himself—were

Mr. Moore's house, where the surrender negotiations were held, still stands today.

present in Yorktown and insisted that Cornwallis be given the same treatment.

The negotiations took so long that the two sides eventually broke it off for the evening and agreed to continue the next day. Washington extended the cease-fire period but kept his men at the ready all night.

Even with the difficult proceedings, the mood on the battlefield had relaxed tremendously. The British, French, and American bands took turns playing songs while they waited. At one point, negotiations became so frenzied that messengers scurried back and forth between the two camps without the formality of waving the white flag or playing the drums.

Finally, after a day and a half of tense discussions, the last details were worked out. Washington would not allow the British to march with their flags flying, but playing music would be permitted. The allies could afford to be a little generous.

᷾

NEWS OF THE SURRENDER spread so quickly that people from all over the Chesapeake Bay region raced to Yorktown. By noon on October 19, a good-sized crowd had gathered to verify that the British army had been defeated.

At 2:00 P.M. sharp, the march began. On one side of the Williamsburg road stood the French in their brilliant white uniforms with white silk flags, the French emblem blazing in gold. On the other side stood the Americans, many of whom lacked uniforms, flags, or shoes. Washington and the other generals were at the end of the line, waiting for their vanquished adversary to come out. The only prominent player missing the ceremony on the allied side was de Grasse, who, suffering from an asthma attack, had sent de Barras to stand in his place.

Slowly the British began to emerge from the tattered city of Yorktown. Most accounts have their band playing a tune called "The World Turned Upside Down," a British nursery rhyme set to a march. The last two lines of the song are, *If summer were spring and the other way 'round / Then all the world would be upside down.*

The Redcoats, though beaten, looked as dashing as the French. Their uniforms were bright and new, their guns polished, their numerous buckles shining. (Anything of value left behind was sure to be confiscated by the allies, so Cornwallis decided the men should wear all they could.) As they marched between the rows of troops, the Redcoats refused to look at the Americans, keeping their eyes on the French instead. This disrespect angered Lafayette, and he ordered the American band to play "Yankee Doodle," which infuriated the British. They glared sullenly at the Americans from then on.

When the first group of prisoners came abreast of Washington, the allied generals learned that Cornwallis had not shown up. He had said he was sick and sent his second in command, Charles O'Hara, for the traditional handing over of the sword.

On a field full of thousands of people, there was not a single sound as O'Hara rode up to Rochambeau. (The British and French had been fighting for so many decades that nearly every officer knew the other in both armies.) O'Hara extended the sword to Rochambeau, but the French general nodded toward Washington. "We are subordinate to the Americans," he said.

O'Hara paused a moment, then rode over to Washington and for a second time extended the sword in the ritual of surrender. Again, there is no record of what the commander in chief was thinking or feeling at that moment. Mounted on his horse, he was nearly the tallest single figure on the battlefield. Every eye was on him. Every soldier was waiting. This would be his crowning moment.

To the astonishment of everyone—especially O'Hara—he refused the sword.

"Never from such a good hand," Washington said. If Cornwallis wasn't going to deliver it himself, then the sword would go to Benjamin Lincoln, O'Hara's equivalent in rank. No matter how hard he'd fought, no matter how much the suffering, the disappointments, and the hardships meant to him, Washington showed he could play the game as well as his European counterparts. Even in victory, the commander in chief was unflappable.

The sword finally accepted, the British were ordered to march to the center of the field and lay down their weapons. It was during this process that several of the allies began to notice that the British soldiers, as they put it, "appeared much in liquor." The

The sword ritual at Yorktown has been an issue of controversy among historians, with some arguing that Benjamin Lincoln never actually took the sword from O'Hara as Washington watched, but merely touched it to signify acceptance.

Redcoats had raided all the available alcohol in Yorktown. As they gave up their weapons, they began slamming their guns on the ground, trying to break the locks and ruin the firing mechanisms. A few minutes was all it took before one of the American generals put a stop to it.

Drunk or sober, the Redcoats began facing up to the reality of what was happening. One Redcoat wrote: "We . . . were staggered by the multitude of those who had besieged us. We were just a guard-mounting in comparison with them, and they could have eaten us up with their power." There was going to be a lot of explaining to do back in England.

Cornwallis was already preparing to defend his part. He wrote to Clinton, saying, "I have the mortification to inform Your Excellency that I have been forced to give up the posts of York and Gloucester and to surrender the troops . . . as prisoners of war to the combined forces of America and France." A few lines later, he insisted, "I never saw this post Yorktown in a favorable light." The finger-pointing among the British was merely beginning.

That night, after the guns had been surrendered and the British troops herded off to prison camps, the main officers from the three armies, following an eighteenth-century custom, sat down and had dinner. The French and English chatted as if they were long lost friends, discussing the multitude of European wars they'd fought in.

Some of the Americans were not happy about the new cordiality. Since 1775, they'd been paying for this moment with the lives of thousands of men. Hatred and ill will had built up over those years, fueled by atrocities on both sides that would be hard to forget.

Having a dinner party was not the ceremony the Americans had in mind.

To top it off, the British still treated them scornfully, considering them not worthy of respect. One French soldier wrote of the British attitude, "They had not even made a handsome defense, and, at this very moment, were beaten and disarmed by peasants who were almost naked, whom they pretended to despise and who, nevertheless, were their conquerors." A Hessian soldier, impressed with the colonists' accomplishments, said, "Out of this rabble has risen a people who defy kings."

Washington said little at these parties. He continued to monitor the countless details involved in making sure the surrender was carried out properly. He was hoping he could talk de Grasse into staying a little longer so that he could sail down to Charleston and retake that city from the British. To his mind, the war was still very much alive.

De Grasse had other plans, however, and began preparing to leave the Chesapeake. Washington had no need to worry. Although he didn't know it at the time, Yorktown would prove the decisive victory of the Revolution.

AT 2:30 A.M. ON OCTOBER 24, a messenger made it to Philadelphia with news of the battle for the Continental Congress. The messenger was knocking on the door of Independence Hall so hard and shouting so loudly that he was nearly arrested by a night watchman before he could get his story out. Once he managed to make himself clear, the city went wild. Fireworks, dancing, drinking, bell-ringing, and feasts commenced

immediately. The whole city was lit up with candles in celebration of the triumph at Yorktown.

It was also on the morning of October 24 that the belated British
rescue mission under Clinton showed up outside Chesapeake Bay,
searching anxiously for the location of de Grasse and his fleet. They
made a startling discovery: Cornwallis and the British army were
prisoners of war.

After discussing their options, the British turned around and
sailed back to New York without firing a single shot.

The last shots of the Revolution had already been fired. Once
reports of the battle reached London, the war effort quickly unrav-
eled. Admiral Hood called the defeat the "most melancholy news
Great Britain ever received." Initially King George tried to deny
the reality of the situation, asserting that Yorktown would not
cause the "smallest alteration in those principles of my conduct
which have directed me in past time." He wanted to double his
efforts to destroy the rebels.

But the British people had had enough. The country was 40
million pounds in debt and fighting wars on four fronts. Most of
the King's advisers were soon forced to resign. The entire government was on the verge of collapse. The King was upset
enough that he wrote a note threatening to abdicate his throne
if the war didn't go on. The note, however, was never delivered,
and finally the British Parliament passed a resolution calling it
treason for anyone to even suggest the war should continue. A
team was assembled to represent Britain in the coming treaty
negotiations. The thirteen colonies were lost forever.

Back in New York, Clinton was relieved of his command and replaced with another general whose only orders were to begin organizing the withdrawal of troops once the treaty was signed. Clinton became miserable, blaming everybody but himself. One British general wrote, "He is a distressed man, looking for friends and suspicious of all mankind, and complains of the number of his enemies. . . . I pity him in his disgrace." Although he was only one part of the failure, it was Clinton who was faulted the most for the British disaster.

On the other hand, Cornwallis revived his fortunes almost instantly. While the press, politicians, and general population went after Clinton, Cornwallis was treated sympathetically. He was sent to India shortly afterward. When he retired, it was with full honors. Yorktown became for him a small black mark on what was otherwise considered a brilliant career.

For its part, the French government didn't fare well after the Revolution, either. By the time the conflict was over, the French treasury was bankrupt. King Louis XVI had spent his country's money on a war that began the age of democratic governments and that would very soon set France aflame in its own revolution—ultimately costing King Louis his head.

Another problem for France was that once it became clear the British were going to grant their independence, the Americans began to abandon their ally. Benjamin Franklin and the other diplomats had promised that they would not negotiate a peace treaty without French participation. Nevertheless, they broke that promise right away. The Americans trusted France as little as they trusted England.

Not that it mattered to the French. They had already begun holding secret meetings with both the British and Spanish during the negotiations in an effort to keep the new nation they'd just helped liberate confined to existing territorial boundaries. The whole process bogged down, with each side accusing the other of false intentions. Negotiations repeatedly floundered and stalled.

Eventually, however, the points were resolved and a treaty acknowledging independence was signed on September 3, 1783. America had finally gained its independence.

⌒

FOR THE NEW COUNTRY called the United States of America, the glory of Yorktown faded fast. The Americans learned that fighting a revolution was one thing; organizing, running, and maintaining a country was another battle altogether.

The most immediate crisis was paying the Continental Army. The way Congress treated the soldiers was scandalous. Not only were most unpaid, but it was also becoming increasingly clear that they would never be paid. A number of young officers made plans to get rid of Congress and start their own government, since the current one didn't seem to care about them at all.

Washington made a fiery speech to his officers, pleading with them not to throw away in an instant what had taken eight hard years to build. He agreed that Congress was treating the army poorly, but to overthrow the new government would go against everything the Revolution stood for.

Because their beloved commander in chief had asked, the officers agreed to wait. One of many crises facing the new nation had narrowly been averted.

For his part, Washington was ready for a rest. Once the treaty was signed and independence declared, he made his final tour of the country as commander in chief, ready to resign his post and go back to Virginia. At every stop along his way, huge crowds gathered to celebrate. It was an exhilarating experience for Washington, bolstering even higher his confidence in the new nation. He wrote: "Heaven has crowned its America other blessings by giving it the fairest opportunity for political happiness than any other nation has ever been favored with, and the result must be a nation which would have a meliorating influence on all mankind."

When he reached New York City, now absent of Redcoats, it was time to say good-bye to his fellow officers. They met at a tavern in the city for an emotional ceremony and dinner.

Afterward, weary and eager to get home, Washington headed for his last stop: Philadelphia and the Continental Congress, where he could step down from the command he'd been given eight years earlier. "Happy in the confirmation of our independence and sovereignty," he said during his speech, "I resign . . . commending the interests of our dearest country to the Protection of Almighty God."

From there, it was to Mount Vernon, and—so he thought—peace and quiet. He wrote to Lafayette, "I am not only retired from all public employments, but I am retiring within myself, and shall be able to view the solitary walk and tread the paths of life with heartfelt satisfaction. . . . I will move gently down the stream of life until I sleep with my fathers."

The farewell dinner with his officers was one of the most emotional moments of Washington's life. One officer present wrote: "Such a scene of sorrow and weeping I had never before witnessed. The simple thought that we were then about to part from the man who had conducted us through a long and bloody war, and under whose conduct the glory and independence of our country had been achieved, and that we should see his face no more in this world, seemed to me utterly insupportable."

Unfortunately, his peace and quiet didn't last long, for a few years later the nation was calling on the architect of the Yorktown success for another duty, this as the first President of the United States.

Once again, Washington, who is still criticized by some historians as a poor strategist, was the right man for the job. This "poor strategist," who fought in only nine battles during the entire Revolution and won just three, understood what was truly needed. It wasn't about strategy. It was about endurance, belief, and commitment to a cause.

That commitment is what led him to take the chance on the journey that brought him to the battle of Yorktown. That victory proved to a skeptical world that there was no way to drive the idea of democracy from the hearts and minds of the colonists. As Patrick Henry said early on in the struggle, "They cannot conquer an idea with an army." As long as Washington led the charge, that idea would never die.

On October 20, the day after the British had thrown down their guns in Surrender Field, Lafayette wrote to a friend in Paris, saying, "The play, sir, is over." As far as the British and French were concerned, it was over. They soon shifted their attention to other parts of the world.

But to George Washington, the play was just beginning.

Pages 142–143:
The inauguration on April 30, 1789, of George Washington as the President of the United States.

Appendix A

BATTLESHIPS OF THE REVOLUTION

The wooden battleships of the Revolutionary era were the undisputed kings of the sea. In England, shipbuilding was the largest single industry. In spite of Britain's overall naval dominance, other European powers, particularly France and Spain, had momentarily surpassed the British in certain areas of design, so that their boats were lighter and easier to maneuver—a development that would hurt the British during the Revolutionary War.

The British had just perfected the technique of sheathing the hull in copper to protect it and to make the boat faster. The innovation was important, as the boats were subject to all sorts of fungi and sea creatures making their homes in the hull, inevitably rotting the wood. This could be a serious problem during wartime, because a damaged ship could take anywhere from three months to two years to repair.

The ships that engaged in battle were called ships of the line. These ships were further divided into categories determined by the ship's size and number of cannons. A first-rate ship, like de Grasse's *Ville de Paris*, had several decks, three of which carried the 110 cannons. The bigger the ships were, however, the harder they were to maneuver. The bulk of most fleets were smaller, carried fewer cannons (70 to 80), and were the most engaged during battle.

Each deck on the ship had its particular function, from storage to sleeping quarters (for everyone except the captain, this usually meant a hammock strung just under the ceiling) to the galley. Only the uppermost decks got any real light. Most of the lower decks had gun ports for windows, and these frequently had to be shut during bad weather or rough seas. The lower you went in the ship, the darker, damper, and more uncomfortable the accommodations became.

- **Ships' Cannons** The number and poundage of cannons were important factors in determining how powerful a battleship could be, but just as critically, the skill of the crew handling the heavy guns often made the difference between victory and defeat. A good crew could get off close to four shots in five minutes. The process of firing cannons varied with equipment and among the navies, but each person in the crew had a specific role to play, from loading to aiming to firing. The big guns of the day, called thirty-two-pounders, had a range of about a quarter mile. Gun crews had to practice constantly so that when battle finally came they would get the important first volley off in time and aimed for the right spots.

  The technology involved with cannons changed dramatically during this period, making them safer and easier to fire. The French in particular had crafted their big guns with accuracy in mind. France had always favored a more conservative attack philosophy in order to preserve its smaller fleet. Its targets were the sails and masts, as opposed to the hull, so that their enemies would be unable to maneuver (or chase them) as quickly.

- **Shot from the Cannon** Many people think of cannonballs as the chief element of destruction from cannons, but a number of other equally deadly items were also fired upon the enemy. If you wanted to penetrate a wooden hull, the traditional **roundshot**, which could weigh as much as thirty-two pounds, was the best. Other projectiles were anti–spars and rigging shot, which included **chain shot,** two balls or pieces of balls chained together; the **bar shot,** a cannonball split in half and joined by a metal bar; and the **elongated shot,** two metal cylinders hooked together. The deadliest material came under the heading "anti-personnel shot." **Grapeshot, capister shot,** and **fagot shot** were containers filled with small pieces of metal, wood, and glass designed to penetrate human skin. These gruesome weapons were often the choice when an aggressive captain tried to rake an opponent's bow or stern. Raking, when a ship moved across the front or back of its enemy's ship and shot all the way down the length of the boat, could be especially deadly.

- **Combatants in the Chesapeake** Following is a table containing the names of the British and French warships involved in the Battle of the Chesapeake (September 5, 1781) and the number of cannons each carried. Because of the unique situation, neither fleet was in its usual fighting order. The ships are listed here in their approximate battle positions. Only a percentage of Graves's and de Grasse's ships actually engaged. Historians contend that Hood should have joined the fight no matter what the sailing instructions were from Graves, and that by doing so he may have changed the outcome. Still, it is clear that the French had more firepower, and, perhaps on that day, more willpower as well.

BATTLESHIPS AND THEIR CANNONS

FRENCH	BRITISH
Pluton / 74	Shrewsbury / 74
Marseillais / 74	Intrepid / 64
Bourgogne / 74	Alcide / 74
Diadème / 74	Princessa / 70
Réfléchi / 64	Ajax / 74
Auguste / 80	Terrible / 74
Saint-Esprit / 80	Europe / 64
Caton / 64	Montagu / 74
César / 74	Royal Oak / 74
Destin / 74	London / 90 / (Graves)
Ville de Paris / 104 / (de Grasse)	Bedford / 74
Victoire / 74	Resolution / 74
Sceptre / 74	America / 64
Northumberland / 74	Centaur / 74
Palmier / 74	Monarch / 74
Solitaire / 64	Barfleur / 90 / (Hood)
Citoyen / 74	Invincible / 74
Scipion / 74	Belliqueux / 64
Maganime / 74	Alfred / 74
Hercule / 74	
Languedoc / 80	
Zélé / 74	
Hector / 74	
Souverain / 74	

- **A Continental Navy?** One delegate at the Continental Congress responded to the suggestion of a Continental Navy as "The maddest idea in the world." Yet during the Revolution, the Americans somehow managed to put together a small collection of ships it called a navy. The navy's goal was not to challenge the British battleships nor directly support Washington's war effort but to focus instead on harassing and disrupting England's sea commerce and cutting down on London's growing source of revenue. It is estimated that the loosely organized combination of official American ships and less official privateers captured almost 2200 British trade vessels. The impact on the British economy was serious enough that British merchants were among the first in England to want the war ended.

༂

WEAPONRY OF THE REVOLUTION

The Revolutionary War era saw major advancements in the field of weaponry, particularly with the cannons and muskets. Although more men died from diseases and infections from wounds than they did from actually being shot, it was clear that the weapons of war would play a bigger role in the conflicts of the future.

- **Land Cannons** Like their counterparts on the warships, cannons on the land were a major factor in the outcome of battles. At a siege like Yorktown, the role the big guns played is more obvious. But the fact is that cannons of one type or another were involved in almost every battle of the Revolution.

  The cannons on land could be larger and more mobile than those at sea (see Appendix A). However, the crew it took to operate them

The American cannoneers, like everyone else in the army, spent more time moving into position and waiting for battles to begin than in actual combat.

had to be just as highly skilled. The troops in the artillery were among the best trained and best drilled in the army. Ironically, they were also the least used to working under musket fire, so that when the enemy infantry broke through the range and the bullets got close, the artillery men were sometimes the first to leave the battle-field—at a run.

Aiming the cannons was easier on land than it was at sea. The troops needed an experienced eye, but there were also tables they could refer to with the various angles that corresponded to the gun's capacity. Elevating the gun to the proper level meant jamming pieces of wood called quoins underneath the breech. All of this required exhausting study and practice to actually pull off during battle.

The cannons of the day fell into three broad categories: **guns,** which had long narrow bodies that fired shot at high speed; **howitzers,** which were shorter and fatter and hurled shells at slower speeds but at higher elevations to get over obstacles; and **mortars,** which were shorter and fatter still and fired shot much higher to get over fort walls and breastworks. Almost all artillery action involved a combination of the three gun types.

Powerful though they were, cannons had a couple of significant drawbacks, the biggest being that they were heavy and difficult to move. Inevitably either oxen or horses were needed to pull the big-ger guns, and during the Revolution that meant traveling over terri-ble mud-soaked roads, or no roads at all.

The other problem was once they were in place, there they stayed. It was too hard to move them during the heat of battle. They gener-ally were either clustered together or spread out across a large area. Once the enemy soldiers got close enough that they were under the

Infantry training manuals were packed with precise drawings like the ones shown here to help the men understand how the weapons should be fired.

guns' ranges, they no longer needed to worry about them and could focus on killing the troops firing the cannons instead.

In spite of these limitations, cannons were a mainstay of the battlefield. There's no question that Washington's strategy for using them at Yorktown hastened Cornwallis's decision.

- **Muskets** There were many steps involved in loading an eighteenth-century musket. Musket drills had to be practiced constantly so that a soldier could complete the multistep procedure in twenty seconds or less—all while enemy bullets hurtled around him. The process seems almost absurd by today's standards. Yet the soldiers of the era had developed routines that turned the musket into a deadly weapon when used effectively.

The English musket of choice was the "Brown Bess." The forty-two-inch-long gun was brass mounted, making it fairly heavy (fourteen pounds). The Americans used the Brown Bess extensively at the beginning of the war, since those were the easiest for them to get.

Once the French joined, however, the Americans switched guns. The French musket was similar to the Brown Bess, only stronger and lighter. The French brought huge numbers of these muskets with them for the Americans.

The classic American-made gun before the war was the long rifle. Unfortunately, it was too slow to load and couldn't hold a bayonet, and was therefore not much use in combat. However, its accuracy at long ranges, much to the dismay of British soldiers who frequently felt safely out of target, was remarkable.

- **Bayonets** The bayonet, a long knife designed to fit over the rifle barrel, was a weapon the colonists had not seen much of before the war started. The first few times the British wielded them during battle had caused panic in the American troops. In close quarters, a soldier skilled with a bayonet could be deadly. More importantly, from Washington's standpoint, the bayonet represented a psychological factor that the superior Redcoats could hold over his less experienced troops. He kept pushing his armies to get bayonets, learn to use them, then stand down the British. By the war's end, the Continental Army had become proficient at using the bayonet, something the British witnessed for themselves at Yorktown.

At the battle of Camden, South Carolina, the British used bayonets with deadly efficiency. It took almost the entire Revolution before Washington's army became accustomed to using the bayonet in battle.

- **Ferguson's Rifle** British Captain Patrick Ferguson (1744–1780) was gunned down at Kings Mountain for his attacks in the Southern colonies, but he'd already made his mark on another aspect of the Revolution: his invention of the first breech-loading rifle used by the British army. Not only was this weapon extremely accurate, but it was also much more dependable in wet weather than the old flint-locks the Americans used. It could also be fired six times in one minute. Fortunately for the Americans, however, the British high command inexplicably failed to follow up on the invention and didn't widely distribute it to the troops.

Appendix C

&

UNIFORMS OF THE REVOLUTION

*I*t is difficult to adequately cover the amazing range of uniforms worn by the multitudes of ranks, divisions, and regiments in the Revolution. There is a tendency to associate red with the British, white with the French, and blue with the Americans, but the reality is much more complicated.

Generally, the armies were comprised of three main parts: the infantry, the cavalry, and the artillery. The infantry represented the bulk of the foot soldiers, the cavalry represented soldiers on horseback (although some divisions were unmounted), and the artillery were the men who managed the gunnery. Each of the groups had distinct uniforms, and within those groups were many variations.

- **French** The British had beaten the French so soundly in the French and Indian War (1754–1763) that it had taken France fifteen years to rebuild its armed forces. But once they were ready, the American Revolution gave France an excellent opportunity to again challenge their hated rivals.

  A side benefit of the rebuilding effort had been a change and standardization in uniforms. While it is hard to specify an exact uniform for the various regiments and divisions, the basic coat and pants color was white, with some officers wearing either dark blue or light blue jackets. The lapels, cuffs, collars, and buttons came in colors designated by the region from which the troops came. These "facing colors" could be anything from silver-gray to violet to crimson. The plumes in the French three-corner hat, which had impressed the Americans during the march to Yorktown, had actually been abolished, but they were popular with many French soldiers and worn in spite of the ban.

- **British** While everyone recognizes the famous red coats of the British, not all the British dressed the same. The blazing coats were definitely the predominant feature, but the color of the lapels, hats, collars, and cuffs varied by region and rank. Many of the soldiers also sported bright white goatskin knapsacks.

  Uniforms also varied to reflect the makeup of the army. One third of the British forces in America during the Revolution was made up of German mercenaries (called Hessians after the region in Ger-

American and French uniforms

many from which many of them hailed). During the war, nearly 20,000 Loyalists were recruited from the colonies, and they, too, had various uniforms.

Much has been made of the supply shortages suffered by the Americans during the war, but the British had supply problems as well. Fighting 3,000 miles from home in a land where they were not welcome made for a difficult job. The lack of timely and reliable supplies was a constant source of frustration for the British army and eventually became a contributing factor in their defeat. They also suffered from the general geography: a soldier carrying everything he was supposed to according to British regulations was loaded down with sixty pounds of equipment. That weight made covering the immense country of America a daunting task indeed.

A British Grenadier in full uniform

- **Americans** The world had never seen an army quite like the one the Americans assembled for the Revolution. Unlike the professional soldiers and mercenaries serving France and Britain, the Continental Army was composed of a wide range of people: from boys barely old enough to carry a gun to grandfathers; from hunters to librarians and scholars; from peasants and craftsmen to merchants and wealthy businessmen. Most had little real military experience, and even if they did, it sometimes mattered little in a conflict that engendered a new kind of military thinking. Henry Knox, who became so skilled at handling heavy artillery that even the British were impressed, had never fired a war cannon before the Revolution. All he knew he had learned from reading books.

  Also unlike most of their European counterparts, American generals wouldn't hesitate to join in a battle if the situation required it. Benedict Arnold did twice at Saratoga, and even Washington himself raced onto the field aboard his white horse to rally the troops at Monmouth Court House.

  Given this unusual mixture of personnel and circumstances, it was almost impossible to standardize uniforms. During the war, Congress made four major attempts to standardize and provide uniforms to its armies, but none of their efforts was especially successful.

  Part of the problem was that Congress had little authority over the thirteen colonies. Although the Continental Army was the largest unit, there were numerous other smaller armies made up of colonial and regional troops. Each colony had its own style of uniform, yet even within the various colonies consistency was lacking. The Continentals frequently sported several colors. Blue was the most common, but green, gray, brown, yellow, and even red could be

*T*he call to arms in Boston and other parts of New England had men rushing away from their farms and families wearing the uniforms that immortalized them as "Minutemen."

found. When a group did get uniforms during the war, it was a certainty that by the time winter came the uniforms would be in tatters. In spite of the clothing regulations Washington tried to put in place, a lot of men ended up wearing fringed hunting shirts and leather leggings or overalls—the classic dress of the minutemen.

The one time that the Continental Army looked at least a little coordinated was at Yorktown. Washington was unwavering in his demand that the army look as good as they could next to their French counterparts in what was going to be a big moment. There was still a large portion without shoes or complete uniforms when Cornwallis's army marched out, but Washington was satisfied that his men looked like "a proper army."

- **Hair Care** As if soldiers didn't have to put up with enough in the Revolution, they were often ordered to powder their hair, as Washington did before his men marched from Williamsburg to Yorktown. Men powdered their hair by first coating their heads with a mixture of lard and candle wax, then topping that off with a thick coat of flour. It's not clear what would happen to this "tonic" after several hours in the hot sun, but it couldn't have been pleasant. Wearing a wig may have sounded good by comparison. Unfortunately, men were discouraged from wearing wigs—unless they were officers.

- **Music Corps** Music was very important to the armies of the Revolution, and not just to keep a beat for marching. Full bands, although rare, were used for boosting morale and for entertainment. But almost all armies had a drum and fife corp. The primary duty of the corps was to pound out the signals and commands during battle, since human voices were nearly impossible to hear above the deafening din of muskets and cannons. The music corps often wore uniforms with opposite color patterns from the rest of the regiments so that the commanding officers could find them quickly.

BIBLOGRAPHY

*T*here are many excellent books written about the American Revolution. The ones listed here are highly recommended, as is the video series *Liberty! The American Revolution* (1997) from PBS Home Video.

Alden, John R. *A History of the American Revolution*. New York: De Capo Press, Inc., 1969.

Bailyn, Bernard. *The Ideological Origins of the American Revolution*. Cambridge: Harvard University Press, 1967.

Battles and Leaders of the American Revolution. Conshohocken, Pa.: Eastern Acorn Press, 1985.

Billias, George A. (editor). *George Washington's Generals and Opponents*. New York: De Capo Press, Inc., 1994.

Bliven, Bruce, Jr. *The American Revolution*. New York: Random House, 1986.

Boatner, Mark M. *Encyclopedia of the American Revolution*. Mechanicsburg, Pa.: Stackpole Books, 1994.

Brookhiser, Richard. *Founding Father: Rediscovering George Washington*. New York: Free Press, 1996.

Carrington, Henry B. *Battles of the American Revolution 1775–1781*. New York: Promontory Press, 1877.

Davis, Burke. *The Campaign that Won America*. Conshohocken, Pa.: Eastern Acorn Press, 1970.

Ferrel, Robert H., and Richard Natkiel. *Atlas of American History*. New York: Facts on File, 1987.

Grafton, John. *The American Revolution—A Picture Sourcebook*. New York: Dover Publications, 1975.

Lancaster, Bruce. *The American Revolution*. Boston: Houghton Mifflin Company, 1987.

Langguth, A. J. *Patriots*. New York: Simon & Schuster, 1989.

Larrabee, Harold A. *Decision at the Chesapeake*. New York: Clarkson N. Potter, Inc., 1964.

McEvedy, Colin. *The Penguin Atlas of North American History*. London: Penguin Books, 1988.

Middlekauff, Robert. *The Glorious Cause*. Oxford: Oxford University Press, 1982.

Mitchell, Joseph B. *Military Leaders in the American Revolution*. McLean, Va.: EPM Publications, 1967.

Morrill, Dan L. *Southern Campaigns of the American Revolution*. Baltimore: The Nautical and Aviation Publishing Company of America, Inc., 1993.

Scheer, George F., and Hugh F. Rankin. *Rebels and Redcoats*. New York: De Capo Press, Inc., 1957.

Symonds, Craig L. *A Battlefield Atlas of the American Revolution*. Baltimore: The Nautical and
     Aviation Publishing Company of America, Inc., 1986.
Tuchman, Barbara W. *The First Salute*. New York: Ballantine Books, 1988.
Wood, W. J. *Battles of the Revolutionary War 1775-1781*. New York: De Capo Press, Inc., 1995.

ILLUSTRATION CREDITS

INDEX